Life After Work

Retirement is a comma in our lives, not a full stop. *Life After Work* looks at the psychological, emotional and wellbeing issues that surround this complex and important transition in life. This book suggests that retirement is a life stage over which we may have greater control than previously thought; it no longer has to be the case that retirement is a terminal point, a time where you became sedentary and inactive.

Retirement is on one level a private, individual matter that affects one's sense of self and purpose, physical and mental processes, as well as financial security or provision. On another level, retirement has an impact on relationships with loved ones, family and friends, as well as colleagues. It can strengthen or disrupt bonds, leading to new bonds being formed or to withdrawal. This book is written by successful authors and psychologists Robert Bor, Carina Eriksen and Lizzie Quarterman, each with many years' experience of helping people cope with life stage changes and prepare for retirement. It contains illustrative case studies throughout, from which valuable lessons can be learned, and draws on the very latest psychological research and techniques to provide a blueprint for planning and living a wonderful retirement or life post-work.

Planning for your future is crucial in enabling you to maximise the opportunities available. Following the book's blueprint will help you prepare for this phase in your life, and the sooner you start the better. *Life After Work* will be of great interest to readers of all ages seeking guidance on retirement and will also appeal to psychologists of life stage changes.

Professor Robert Bor is a Consultant Psychologist at the Royal Free Hospital and also in private practice as Dynamic Change Consultants as well as the Centre for Aviation Psychology. He works at Leaders in Oncology Care, the London Clinic, St Paul's School, the Royal Ballet School, the Royal Air Force and several UK airlines. He divides his time between London and the Cotswolds, and has young twins and a cocker spaniel.

Dr Carina Eriksen is a registered and chartered Consultant Counselling Psychologist. She runs a busy private practice in central London, Chelsea and the City. She is a fellow at the BPS, a BPS board committee member in aviation psychology and a BABCP accredited therapist. She is married with two young children.

Lizzie Quarterman lives on a National Trust farm in Gloucestershire with her husband and several characterful cocker spaniels. She grows vegetables and paints landscapes, and in professional life is an experienced writer and editor of business and psychology books and articles.

Life After Work

A Psychological Guide to a Healthy Retirement

Robert Bor, Carina Eriksen and Lizzie Quarterman

LONDON AND NEW YORK

First published 2019
by Routledge
2 Park Square, Milton Park, Abingdon, Oxon OX14 4RN

and by Routledge
52 Vanderbilt Avenue, New York, NY 10017

Routledge is an imprint of the Taylor & Francis Group, an informa business

© 2019 Robert Bor, Carina Eriksen and Lizzie Quarterman

The right of Robert Bor, Carina Eriksen and Lizzie Quarterman to be identified as authors of this work has been asserted by them in accordance with sections 77 and 78 of the Copyright, Designs and Patents Act 1988.

All rights reserved. No part of this book may be reprinted or reproduced or utilised in any form or by any electronic, mechanical, or other means, now known or hereafter invented, including photocopying and recording, or in any information storage or retrieval system, without permission in writing from the publishers.

Trademark notice: Product or corporate names may be trademarks or registered trademarks, and are used only for identification and explanation without intent to infringe.

British Library Cataloguing-in-Publication Data
A catalogue record for this book is available from the British Library

Library of Congress Cataloging-in-Publication Data
A catalog record has been requested for this book

ISBN: 978-1-138-33583-7 (hbk)
ISBN: 978-1-138-33585-1 (pbk)
ISBN: 978-0-429-44351-0 (ebk)

Typeset in Times New Roman
by Taylor & Francis Books

Contents

List of tables	ix
Foreword	x
About the authors	xii

Introduction	1
1 The changing face of retirement	3

   What is retirement? 3
   Why has retirement changed? 5
      Longevity 5
      Health advances 6
      Government encouragement to offset demographic
         change 7
      Higher standard of living 9
      Higher cost of living 10
   Identification 10

2 Psychological perspectives	12

   Why is psychology relevant? 12
   Assumptions 13
   Impact of thoughts 14
      Negative expectations 14
      Positive expectations 15
      Some of the things you may miss 16
   Thinking traps 17
   Fear of change 18

How people react to change 19
Psychological techniques to overcome fear 20
   How to avoid overreacting 20
Factors that affect "healthy" adjustment 22
Emotional instability 23

3   The maturing brain   27

What happens to the mature mind? 27
Mental processing as we age 28
Dementia 29
Keeping your brain fit 30
Common "purposeful" activities 32
Giving back 32
   Volunteering 32
   Become a trustee 34
   Mentoring 34
   Join an altruistic society, or become a fundraiser 35
   Pass on your skills 36
The power of play 36
Use it or lose it 38
More tips for improving your mental health 39

4   Psychological approaches to challenging feelings and
    behaviours   40

Fear, worry and anxiety: thinking errors 41
Strategies for coping with fear, worry and anxiety 41
Cognitive behavioural therapy 45
Thought activation 46
Stress and anxiety management 47
Low mood 48
   Strategies for dealing with low mood 48
Loss, grief and bereavement 49
   Strategies for coping with loss 51
Sleep problems 51
   Strategies for dealing with sleep problems 53
Loneliness 53
   Strategies to help you deal with loneliness 54

Addictions 57
    Strategies for coping with addictions 60

5 Retirement and emotions   63

    Loss 63
    Emotional stress 63
    Low mood 64
    Uncertainty 64
    Unhappiness 64

6 The impact on relationships   66

    The impact 66
    Relationship tips 72
    Develop separateness 72
    Gender, sex and problems 73
    Preventing relationship breakdown and divorce 75

7 Moving on from work   77

    Leaving the workplace 77
    How to retire from self-employment 78
    How to retire from unemployment 80
    What next? 80
        Carry on working 80
        Setting up on your own 81
    Beware the traps 81
        The volunteering trap 82
        The failing to fly the nest trap 82
        The caring trap 82

8 Mind your health   84
    OLIVER PATRICK

    Quick fix for successful ageing 84
    Move 85
    Exercise 86
    Diminishing muscle mass 86

Brain function 90
Food 91
    Mediterranean diet 92
    Balance your blood sugar 92
    Nourish yourself 93
    Eat mindfully 93
    Track yourself 94
Retirement as an opportunity to improve your health 95

9 Mind your money: Financial planning for retirement   96
   MARTIN JONES AND WATERSON JONES

   How much income will you need? 97
   How much capital will you need? 97
   Annuities 99
   What return do you need? 99
   Tax relief and legislation 101
   Money in bricks 101

10 Thoughts on life (after work)   103

11 Bringing it all together: The blueprint for a psychologically sound retirement   107

   Planning ahead 107
   Start saving 107
   Prepare for old age 108
   Your 20-point retirement blueprint 108

Resources   109
Index   112

Tables

4.1 Thomas's reflections about his own situation 58
8.1 Clinically observed features and how to track them at home 94

Foreword

With the possible exception of domestic violence, fatal illnesses, terrorism, global warming, nuclear explosions and death, few topics generate as much anxiety as retirement. In my professional experience, people struggle to think coherently about retirement, because it evokes so many fears about the end of our lives.

Even great psychologists have a difficult time grappling with retirement. Professor Sigmund Freud, though riddled with cancer throughout his late sixties, his seventies and into his early eighties, stopped working with psychoanalytical patients only weeks before his death in 1939. A compulsive worker, Freud never formally retired, as he could not dare to contemplate a life devoid of intense labour.

Many of us fear that, upon retirement, we may not be able to support ourselves or our loved ones and, moreover, that we will have no useful role. We may also fear the loss of the eroticism of our youth. As one of my elderly female patients once remarked, "No one looks at a woman of my age. Whenever I walk down the street, I might as well be invisible." This person resisted retirement because she believed that, having "lost" her looks, she had no other way of feeling useful than by continuing to work in paid employment, in spite of the physical burdens of doing so.

Another one of my psychotherapy patients once opined, "I can never retire. If I do, I might as well dig my own grave and throw myself in."

Happily, Robert Bor, Carina Eriksen and Lizzie Quarterman hold a different viewpoint. Although these psychological authors acknowledge the fears and vulnerabilities associated with retirement, they certainly do not regard it as a death sentence. Quite the contrary, this optimistic trio has come to regard the retirement process as a truly rich opportunity.

In their new book, *Life After Work: A Psychological Guide to a Healthy Retirement*, these positively minded and uplifting specialists provide us with a magnificent guide to the many ways in which retirement might come to be experienced as a marvellous canvas of possibility, rather than as a source of inevitable misery. Throughout these well-written and inspiring chapters, Professor Robert Bor, Dr Carina Eriksen and Lizzie Quarterman have offered us a multitude of creative suggestions for how we can use our post-employment time effectively, even joyfully, painting a portrait of retirement in such exciting terms that I now look forward to my own golden years more than ever before!

The range of options and future directions proposed by these writers can only be described as astounding: becoming trustee of a charity, working as a mentor, volunteering and so forth. Indeed, each page brims with cunning notions and presents the reader with new thoughts and dreams.

Steeped in the practice of psychology, the authors certainly do not idealise the retirement process as one great big party; they recognise, unquestionably, the potential dangers, including the vulnerability to depression and anxiety. But throughout this text, they provide a great sense of hopefulness, recognising that psychological therapies and other forms of social support can help men and women of retirement age to navigate and, ultimately, enjoy some of the internal obstacles that might mitigate against a satisfying post-employment life.

Richly illustrated with clinical case material, this book offers a full and frank portrait of the challenges of retirement. In spite of the difficulties of navigating this chapter of our later lives, the authors remain committed to the philosophy that retirement can be a remarkable time for resolving some of our old conflicts and issues and, also, for developing our creativities and joys in unexpected ways.

I cannot recommend this book highly enough, not only to the older members of the population who may be contemplating retirement at the present time, but also to those younger people who may not even have begun to think about the possibilities that may lie in wait. I would even encourage those who have *already* mastered the art of retirement to study this tome, because it will, undoubtedly, trigger some exciting new ideas.

I congratulate Robert Bor, Carina Eriksen and Lizzie Quarterman, and their guest contributors, for sharing their expertise in such a generous fashion and for enthusing us with their infectious sense of hope and optimism. In having done so, they have made an important contribution to the psychological literature, and they have provided us all with a cheerful roadmap for the future.

Professor Brett Kahr

About the authors

Professor Rob Bor is a Clinical, Counselling and Health Psychologist at the Royal Free Hospital, London, as well as an Aviation Psychologist and Executive Coach. He is also the Consultant Psychologist to the Leaders in Oncology Care – Harley Street, the London Clinic, Blossoms Health Care, St Paul's School, the Royal Ballet School, the Royal Air Force and numerous national and international airlines. He is a partner at Dynamic Change Consultants Ltd (www.dccclinical.com) and the Centre for Aviation Psychology Ltd (www.centreforaviationpsychology.com). He runs retirement preparation seminars for senior executives. He divides his time between Hampstead (London) and the Cotswolds, and has young twins and a cocker spaniel. He doesn't plan to stop working, but making more time for his hobby and sport interests is definitely on his agenda.

Dr Carina Eriksen is a Consultant Psychologist with an extensive London-based private practice for young people, adults, couples and families. She is a Fellow of the British Psychology Society, a registered aviation psychologist and an accredited member of the British Association for Behavioural and Cognitive Psychotherapies. She is an author and a co-author of several books and her work has been published in prestigious scientific journals. She lives in London with her husband and two young children.

Lizzie Quarterman, BA(Hons), is based in the Cotswolds. She has a characterful husband (technically retired but still working as hard as ever), four home-bred cocker spaniels and a grown-up cat. She is a freelance writer and editor of psychology textbooks, academic articles, business books and websites.

Contributors

Martin Jones is a financial consultant based in Kent. Among his past roles, he founded the financial planning and investment company Waterson Jones.

Oliver Patrick is executive director of Viavi, a health management consultancy. He works personally with many leaders in business and high net-worth clients, shaping programmes and supporting them in achieving their health and wellbeing goals.

Introduction

Retirement is a comma in our life, not a full stop. It was previously thought of as a terminal point in your life, a time where you became sedentary and inactive. But this no longer has to be the case. In this book we will look at the psychological, emotional and wellbeing issues that surround this complex and important life stage transition. Unlike other life events, such as illness and redundancy, retirement is one we can prepare for. In this respect, retirement is the one, similar to becoming a parent or committing to a marriage, over which we may have greater control.

Why is a psychologist co-authoring this book? Let's be very clear: we don't see retirement as a mental health problem, but if it is poorly managed and leads to stagnation, regret, withdrawal, low mood or alcoholism it could lead to mental health problems. There is also a psychological element because retirement is a transition point in your life and you do not want to become stuck in this period of transition and be unable to move through it. We want you to be able to look forward to your well-earned retirement.

Retirement may not be a mental health problem, but it can be a big change for you to take on. You will need to move through this period of change and on to the next phase of your life. When you retire, it is from a job, a role, a position ... not from life! When we think of retirement we see it as a process we can prepare for and then move through onto the next thing. You work towards retirement from the very first day you begin work. You have power over it because you can prepare for it.

Retirement is on one level a private, individual matter that affects your sense of self, your purpose in life, your physical and mental processes as well as your financial security or provision. On another level, retirement has an impact on your relationships – with your loved ones, family and friends, as well as with your work colleagues. It can strengthen or disrupt bonds with those around you, and also lead to new bonds being formed or a withdrawal from the social world you inhabit. Valuable lessons can be those learned from counselling professionals who have got stuck, and we feature a number of illustrative case studies throughout the book.

We also draw on the very latest psychological research and techniques in order to provide you with a blueprint for planning and living a wonderful retirement or life post-work. We believe the key point here is preparation. Planning for your future is crucial to enable you to maximise the opportunities available, whether through increased financial freedom due to looking after your finances, increased mobility due to looking after your health or some other forethought. Following our blueprint will help you prepare for this phase in your life, and the sooner you start the better. In fact it is never too early to begin laying down the foundations for your future.

Retirement is not the end of anything, and it is helpful to view the official point of retirement, if indeed there is one, as a comma in your life rather than a full stop. A change of tack. A sidestep. A new phase in your life.

Chapter 1

The changing face of retirement

What is retirement?

Retirement is both an event and a process. It is an event in that at a given moment or date you will stop working or being engaged in a particular activity you have been involved in, in a work or career capacity. This may come about because you have planned and chosen for this to happen or it may be forced upon you due to redundancy, ill health, family and personal circumstances or other reasons. Some people dread the moment and fear the prospect of this important life change; others may welcome or relish the prospect of change in their life and have carefully planned for this eventuality from when they first started working.

Retirement doesn't have to be the end of your working life, or the end of your life as you know it. It can be the start! In this book, we want to help you begin to think about how you want your life to be in the future. With the guidance we suggest, your so-called "retirement" could in fact be the most fulfilling stage of your life, especially as you will now have far more control over how you spend your time than you ever did when you were working.

Whether or not you continue to work in some form, approaching the third stage of your life as an "encore career" – a new phase in your life – is a mentally healthy attitude. Preparing for a new career requires a degree of strategic preparation, and here we give you a blueprint you can follow to make the most of your life after retirement.

Retirement is also a process in that it involves working towards something, running down, handing over and also planning for your next stage of life. Less than a generation ago retirement was seen as an absolute and predictable event. It was absolute because there was a legal retirement age and so it was predictable, in that when you reached a certain point in life you would be obliged to give up your work. This is no longer so – and indeed in the space of less than ten years the whole notion of retirement has been turned on its head.

These days, retirement can happen at almost any point in your working life. It can also occur more than once in your working life. You could be one of the few people for whom it comes sooner, coinciding with good fortune, high earnings and careful planning, allowing you to support yourself financially and in other ways for the rest of your life. For many, the fact that there is no longer a legal requirement to retire can be welcome. It means that you can continue in your role, or in a working capacity, for as long as you are able to perform your job. You may go through a succession of jobs and indeed different careers. It opens up the prospect of variety, change and opportunities. Either way, it can be a time of mixed emotions.

The form retirement takes may differ from the traditional concept or expectation of retirement. Nowadays, it is more likely to be planned, involve activities, and help to achieve fulfilment in your life goals. It is also likely to impact on relationships around you, not only in positive ways, but also at times, in some unwelcome ways.

Maintaining physical and mental wellbeing will be a core focus for many who retire, mindful of increasing longevity and the opportunities and challenges this brings. Careful management of your finances over a longer period, and all the complexity this demands, requires specialist advice and will need a deal of planning. This will be in regard to not only your financial situation and preparing for old age, but also the sensitive issues of preparing for your demise, loss within the family and legal incapacity.

Managed well, retirement can make you feel fulfilled, accomplished and confident, and lead to greater wellbeing and enjoyment. In contrast, not managing the important financial, social, psychological and other aspects to retirement satisfactorily could adversely affect your physical and mental health, your sense of wellbeing and indeed your longevity.

Quite simply, retirement is now a very different entity to what it was less than a generation ago. Planned for carefully, it can be one of the most pleasurable and fulfilling times of your life. However, there are challenges and risks, and this self-help book aims to highlight some of these and to address them in a practical way, based on tried and tested psychological ideas and practical guidance.

However you want to view it, you can navigate the transition more smoothly with careful planning and preparation, and this book is designed to help you with this. If you fail to do this, there is the danger of financial and practical problems caused by a lack of foresight, and potentially psychological problems may ensue, impacting personal wellbeing and relationships. And having a sense of control over when you leave your job will give you a feeling of power over the situation.

This book has been written to help you enhance your sense of wellbeing with regard to retirement planning. We highlight some of the psychological challenges brought about by this important life event and draw attention to many of the emotions that people attribute to retirement and retirement planning. We also look at what happens to us after we retire and how this can affect us mentally and physically. Based on real experiences, research and also tried and tested psychological interventions, we point out some ways in which to prepare for and manage retirement better, or at the very least purposefully and with a clear sense of direction. Left to chance, retirement can be welcome and fulfilling; however, without some planning, it can be a time beset with fear, worry, stress, anxiety, sleepless nights, irritability and stress that finds its way into relationships. In some cases, it can also lead to negative behaviour and lifestyle choices such as consuming too much alcohol, gambling, sedentary time spent on the Internet and the physical and mental health consequences of these behaviours.

We want to help you begin to think about how you want your life to be in the future. With the tips we suggest, your so-called "retirement" could in fact be the most fulfilling stage of your life – you will have far more control over how you spend your time than you ever did when you were working. More and more people are going against the traditional grain, and refusing to accept that their "useful" life is over just because they get to a certain age. First, we look at why this is happening.

Why has retirement changed?

Longevity

We are all living longer, with average life expectancy now age 83 for a woman, 79 for a man, and this increases by 5 hours every day. Medical care and advances in tackling diseases that previously killed many at a younger age mean more of us are living to a greater age. For example, influenza used to be fatal in the majority of cases; almost all of us now recover after a week in bed. A male aged 65 has a 50 per cent chance of reaching the age of 87.

Men and women used to be considered "old" in their forties, and "ancient" after that, especially by the young. Nowadays, people don't consider themselves as "elderly" until their mid-eighties! In 2013 the average age exceeded 40.

> Ask yourself: How do you feel about possibly living to an older age than your parents and grandparents?
> What does "ageing" mean to you? Get a pen and a piece of paper and try to record 5–8 points that come to your mind when you think about getting older. Is there some balance between the welcome and unwelcome ones? How can you address, prepare for or overcome any ideas that may be unwelcome or even troubling? Are you surprised by anything you have noted?

Health advances

We are, on the whole, enjoying better health. Advances in medical research and treatment means most of us are well for longer in our lives. The recent decade has also seen an increase to educational advice on how to maintain a healthy lifestyle by promoting physical exercise, sensible diets and emotional wellbeing. Chronic illnesses are generally better managed and we no longer have to live with minor problems that in the past would have prevented us from working, like cataracts or hip problems.

Our lives are also easier than they were:

- shorter working hours take less of a toll;
- labour-saving devices save energy and effort;
- cars have reduced walking and cycling to get around;
- our homes are more comfortable and warmer;
- advances in technology allows us to pay bills online, work from home and connect socially across the world; and
- we enjoy a far better diet, with more variety and availability.

People used to have to retire when they were worn out, physically unable to continue. Unless you are a manual worker like a dry stone waller, out in all weathers and carrying heavy loads, this is less likely these days.

We all get tired as we get older, but can often continue to work because of the possibilities of reducing our hours by changing shifts, going part-time, job-sharing or working from home. So the prospect of continued working in the same job or some other form of it, or beginning an active retirement, is less often limited by physical debilitation than in the past.

> Ask yourself: Do you think your life is easier than the life your parents and grandparents had at your age?
> What do you see as the benefits (and perhaps also the disadvantages) of modern lifestyles?

However, increasing longevity raises specific opportunities and challenges. Here are some examples:

- finances may come under pressure;
- more health problems may present (some can be treated; some can't);
- longer relationships; this may be a pressure or challenge; and
- interests may wane or fluctuate.

Keeping up with fast paced changes in society may feel more challenging – some people are good at adapting to changes while others may be less able to adjust to new ways of living or thinking.

If we expect to live longer, with improved healthcare, health prevention and lifestyle changes made at an earlier stage in life, we may have more capacity, and more inclination or need, to work. On the other hand, living longer does not mean we can assume sufficiently robust physical and mental health to keep working as we might have done at other stages of our lives. The average cost of a four-year stay in a care home is set to double in the next 20 years. As we will highlight later in this book, maintaining your physical and mental health, as well as sharpness of mind, requires a strategy and purpose and should not be left to chance. Staying psychologically healthy as we age is important for many reasons, but especially because we are more likely to maintain and develop friendship and relationships, which buffer us from stress and improve a sense of wellbeing.

Government encouragement to offset demographic change

In the whole of the Western world the population is ageing. We are living longer, and the birth rate has been declining. The House of Lords Committee on Public Service and Demographic Change, in its 2013 Filkin Report, warns that the government and our society are woefully underprepared for ageing. The committee says that longer lives can be a great benefit, but there has been a collective failure to address the implications. The report concluded that we as a country are nowhere near ready for an ageing population and without urgent action this great boon could turn into a series of miserable crises.

The Filkin Report identifies how England will see an average rise of 51 per cent in those aged 65+ and a 101 per cent increase in those aged 85+ from 2010 to 2030. Interestingly, the East Midlands shows the highest rises, with the figures being 58 per cent and 108 per cent respectably. The comparable figures for London are 46 per cent and 66 per cent.

The UK's ageing population means that unless measures are taken to support working longer the size of the UK's workforce is likely to flatline, projected to increase by only 4.5 per cent over the next two decades, down from 18.2 per cent over the past two decades, according to a Business in the Community report.

This top-heavy demographic causes a number of problems:

- a growing employment gap, with not enough youngsters leaving education to fill the available jobs;
- growing demand on the NHS for hospital beds and care homes, and the staff to run them; and
- increased financial burden on the younger generations to support the elderly.

The issue of an increasing pensions burden as the population ages is a growing one across Europe. The International Longevity Centre–UK (ILC) has published a study into how European countries are tackling demographic change issues, titled *Europe's Ageing Demography*. This report shows that, "as the EU population ages, the level of expenditure on pensions is set to rise significantly. Pension expenditure as a proportion of European GDP is expected to increase by 14.2 per cent in the years leading up to 2060."

The European Commission projects that public spending on long-term care as a proportion of GDP will rise from 1.8 per cent in 2010 to 3.6 per cent by 2060, an increase of 94 per cent, according to Eurostat (https://ec.europa.eu/eurostat).

So, from the government's point of view, there is an urgent need to encourage older workers to stay in work and stay healthy. In particular, the Filkin Report recommended that Government and employers should work to end "cliff-edge" retirement, which is the sudden ending of our working lives, followed by a sedentary life devoid of work, whether paid or unpaid. This is the approach we take in this book as well – as we shall show, a smooth transition into post-retirement life is better for our mental health as well as for our pockets and for the government and welfare services too – a win–win situation.

The ILC's *Europe's Ageing Demography* report states that "Europe as a whole must adapt to a new world where it is projected that almost 1 in 3 people will be over 65, and more than 1 in 10 will be over the age of 80." Basically, governments need to keep people in work for longer. The UK is not alone in abolishing compulsory retirement and raising pension ages: some countries have introduced flexible working, others operate bribe and/or punishment schemes for pension payments. For example, New Zealand introduced a compulsory retirement savings scheme called KiwiSaver in 2007, and Japan has begun to raise the mandatory retirement age. The Swedish approach is to have the unconditional right to work up to the age of 67, two years beyond the date at which the basic state pension could be drawn.

The Department of Work and Pensions has appointed a Business Champion for Older Workers, Ros Altmann, CBE. In 2014, she discussed the government's action plan at the Recruitment & Employment Confederation's meeting on harnessing the potential of older workers. The government is taking this issue extremely seriously.

Higher standard of living

Many of us have parents or grandparents who lived through the war and experienced hardship and rationing. We are considerably more affluent than they were. Despite recent recessions, total income for the retired is higher than ever, at £29,095, with the average household disposable income £17,229 (or £27,807 for those with a private pension) in 2015/16, according to the latest Office of National Statistics figures. Many people earn more than their parents' generation, but it does not necessarily follow that they *feel* more affluent. The cost of living and expectations around lifestyle, for example, can easily drain financial resources.

We may be accustomed to a higher standard of living, and often seek to maintain this for longer. For example, who wants to stop or reduce spending on holidays, meals out, theatre trips, club membership subscriptions, gifts, running a car and so on, particularly at the exact time when one may well have more time to enjoy these things?

> Ask yourself: Consider those aspects of your affluent lifestyle you would like to continue into retirement. Make a list of the most important things you enjoy and prioritise these on a scale from 1 (most important) to 10 (least important). This will help the process of planning your retirement by incorporating positive lifestyle activities. You may also want to add new

> hobbies or activities such as learning to play golf, make jewellery or take an art class.

Higher cost of living

The cost of living is higher and the real value of pension income has fallen. In the UK the state pension is just over 30 per cent of average earnings, according to ILC Europe's Ageing Demography report.

According to the latest Office of National Statistics Consumer Price Index published in June 2018, which measures the cost of living, inflation is now 2.3 per cent., after reaching a high of 2.7 per cent in August 2017. It has been far higher, at 5.2 per cent in 2011, and may well start to rise again with continuing uncertainty and concerns over Brexit, US tariffs and the effect of climate change on food production.

It is important to make arrangements to ensure we have enough money to live well when we retire. Financial stress is very real, and stress of any sort causes decay and degeneration in both body and mind. In a study of 15,000 people in 15 countries, the average extent of retirement in the UK was found to be 19 years; unfortunately, the average person's savings for retirement will last only a third of that time.

The recent recessions gave rise to real hardship for some pensioners, who saw their income from investments drop dramatically over an extended period of time. ILC Europe's Ageing Demography report shows that more than 15 per cent of UK over-65s are at risk of poverty. There are a number of steps that can be taken to offset the risk of this happening, by careful financial planning, and we look at this issue in the next chapter of this book.

> Ask yourself: Do your future financial plans allow for fluctuations in the cost of living?

Identification

When you meet someone new, at a drinks party for instance, invariably the first question they ask is "And what do you do?". We are defined by our jobs, by what we do. We identify with our job titles and the companies we work for. They confer status on us, and define us in a way others can understand.

> Ask yourself: How do I define myself? Draw a circle and divide up the whole into slices, like cutting a cake, and think about the various aspects that define you as a person? You may wish to think about the wider areas of your life such as your family role, personal characteristics or certain abilities. What value do you place on each of these?

The issue of losing your identity, your status, can make it harder for you to actually give up work. This is one reason why traditional retirement is becoming an old-fashioned concept, particularly for professionals who would miss having a career, the English Longitudinal Study on Ageing has found. In fact, 5 per cent of men aged 50–75 are "unretired" – meaning that they tried retirement but decided they would prefer to work. Most were managers or consultants and worked for around 20 hours per week. In addition to this are those who remained in work or did voluntary work.

And according to Christopher Brooks of Age UK, many people "simply enjoy the identification of the workplace so when they stop working they miss it". You may also really enjoy being at work – the camaraderie, the teamwork, the successes and achievements, or the simple act of going out to work away from the home.

> Ask yourself: What will/won't you miss about work or working? How much do you enjoy your job? Would you miss the satisfaction gained from the sense of achievement? Would you miss the sociability? Or the routine? Or the sense of being someone, being defined by the job you do or the company you work for?

So, more of us are in better shape, will live longer, are better off and have higher standards of living that we wish to maintain into our retirement. We crave identification and are more motivated in a number of ways to continue contributing to society.

Chapter 2

Psychological perspectives

Why is psychology relevant?

Retirement is not a psychological problem or disorder! It is merely a life stage transition. However, life stage transitions increase the risk of psychological problems. Each life transition can throw you off because you get anxious about how this transition will be made and this can cause a "tightening up" psychologically. You may fear change, the process or outcome of change, or some aspect of change – such as not being able to precisely predict the outcome. Perhaps you have had unpleasant experiences of change on previous occasions. When this happens, your thoughts and actions can become or may seem "stuck" or predictable. People around you in turn may get closer to engage with you as you go through the ups and downs of change, or they may withdraw or absent themselves. Change therefore has a ripple effect through your family and social network. This does not mean that change will inevitably profoundly destabilise your sense of self and disrupt your ties with others; but it can unsettle us emotionally. And retirement certainly has the ability to unsettle you irrespective of how long you have prepared for it or how much you have anticipated and welcomed it.

Managed well, the transition to retirement can be very positive. It can improve your self-confidence, your sense of attainment and achievement, your sense of self, and your personal happiness. It may also have a positive impact on your relationships allowing you to spend more time with the family, your partner or friends. What's not to like?

However, retirement is also both a personal challenge and an experiment; there is no right or wrong way to do or manage it – in psychological terms, this means it is an individual process. We are all different, and your way of muddling through it is not necessarily the best way for others and vice versa. There are multiple issues involved: lifestyle, financial, emotional, social etc. Your journey to retirement will be influenced by your individual circumstances and is therefore a unique process that you can shape according to your life situation.

> Ask yourself: How ready are you to think outside the box and actively manage your future life rather than just let it happen? What steps do you think you need to consider when planning ahead for your retirement? Are there particular areas you think may be more difficult for you to manage than others? Some people may fear a loss of structure whereas other people may fear financial struggles.

What is it about life transition that can cause psychological constrictions? Around the time of change there may be issues that can worry you, such as what is your legacy? What will happen to your identity and your family? This has a ripple effect on those you are close to. You may tend to become angry or withdraw from others, which will either lead others to become closer to you or they might withdraw from you. People can pull away to protect themselves from your being unsettled by change, or your emotional pain. You can also inadvertently increase the distance between you and your partner in order to protect them.

While undergoing change you can get stuck in this process and this can lead to physical and bodily signs that show you are stressed. A myriad of problems can arise if you don't handle life transitions effectively and settle in to the new patterns with ease.

A psychological approach can help with goal setting; managing personal, couple, family and work changes; and reflecting on life goals. Most importantly, it can help put you in control of this significant life change.

Assumptions

Do you have an image in your mind of a retired cardigan-wearing man in front of a small fire, snoozing over the crossword, or of a shawled woman knitting bed socks with her glasses on the end of her nose? These depict some of the negative preconceptions we have made about our future, based on our older relatives or on rather Dickensian images from the media.

If you ask people at random what they think retirement will be like, they will often say one or more of the following:

- I have to stop work at a certain age.
- I have to downsize to a flat or bungalow.
- My money will be tight.
- I will lose my identity.

- I will need to wear clothes fastened with Velcro.
- I will be bored.
- I won't have a sex life.
- I will suffer ill health and mental decline.
- I will watch a lot of daytime TV.
- I will be lonely.
- I will have to do everything with my partner.
- I will start to like sherry, bingo and bowls.
- I will be in pain.
- I will lose my freedom.
- I will become a ditherer.
- I will be treated with less respect.
- My experience will not be valued.
- I won't have anything to talk about.
- I will become invisible.
- My future will not be bright.
- I will be a widow/widower.

Not exactly an enticing advertisement for retirement, is it?

> Ask yourself: What are you most worried will happen when you become retired? Make a list of the assumptions you hold and ask yourself "to what degree are these assumptions a reflection of my worry and to what degree are they likely to happen?"

Impact of thoughts

Your habitual thoughts will impact reality. Which is better: "Retirement will be boring" or "Retirement will be an adventure"? We have facilitated retirement seminars and individual sessions with thousands of people – whether young or older – planning for retirement or going through the process, and also with those who have already retired. Common worries, dilemmas and pleasures are often raised and discussed. Some of the ideas are summarised below, as they offer a window into the ups - and downs – of retirement as perceived by many others.

Negative expectations

The top six negative expectations associated with retirement shared with us by those planning their retirement are as follows:

Psychological perspectives 15

1 Being unlinked from a work context that affords structure, identity, a role, regular income and meets some of my social and afflictive needs.
2 Being viewed by others – including within my own family – as elderly or old.
3 Spending inordinate amounts of time at home with not enough to keep me busy.
4 Being more with my partner and feeling stressed at the thought that this may upset the balance in our relationship by intruding into one another's space.
5 Worrying about finances and managing expenses over whatever time lies ahead.
6 Feeling a sense of uselessness, lack of drive or lack of accomplishment without work.

Positive expectations

On the plus side, there are lots of positive things about retirement to focus on. Here are some of the things people say:

- Feeling more in control of my life.
- Looking forward to the continuation of friendships formed at work that will be sustained through retirement.
- Having space to do my own thing.
- Being able to fill my own time.
- Freedom to have a social life that does not necessarily have limits.
- To start living the way I have been dreaming about.
- An opportunity to lead a more flexible life without a sense of control or being bossed around.
- Being able to travel where and when I wish.
- Being able to go back and study on a course or for a degree that I've always wanted to pursue.
- Learning new skills.
- Open up new social networks and making new friends.
- More time spent with my family and grandchildren.
- More control over my diary.
- Moving abroad to discover another culture, alternative way of living.

And some things are good to leave behind! You'll no longer:

- have to deal with office politics and operating procedures that feel constraining;
- hear the moaning and gossip;

- feel accountable and "tagged" by your work;
- have unreasonable demands placed on you;
- experience the stress of work deadlines;
- receive text messages and emails from work colleagues over the weekend or in the evenings;
- have to deal with your boss; and
- commute to work and be stuck in traffic jams or overcrowded trains.

> Ask yourself: What are you most looking forward to about retiring? Can you make a plan on how to best incorporate these aspects into your life for when you retire?

By the way, one thing to watch out for is the "honeymoon" period (commonly the first year of retirement) – you might experience exhilaration with your new-found freedom. But this feeling may wane and emotional stability may be threatened, so it is important to plan ahead to guard against this.

Some of the things you may miss

Leaving your job may not be all good. Here are some of the things people say they miss about leaving work:

- particular people and colleagues I worked with;
- having an assistant or PA to help support me and help manage my life;
- having younger people around to teach or mentor;
- having a purpose when I get up in the morning;
- being in situations where I successfully solve work-related problems;
- having status;
- my daily routine;
- being challenged intellectually;
- the income;
- feeling wanted or needed;
- the perks from work;
- the recognition and respect from colleagues;
- the opportunities to socialise; and
- the sense of belonging to a group, especially for those who work in teams.

> Ask yourself: What do you think you might miss when you leave work? Is there an alternative or new aspect you wish to pursue when you retire that can bridge a gap between what you are missing and "new pleasure".

Thinking traps

The previous negative preconceptions are based on a series of assumptions we have made, often subconsciously, that are called "thinking traps" or "thinking errors".

Are you a worrier? Worry can often lead us to look at a situation from a catastrophic angle where we may convince ourselves of the worst possible outcome in a given situation. Worry can often be triggered by uncertainty or the unknown. The process of worry can often have a positive intention where we try to "predict", "solve" or create some sense of certainty during periods of uncertainty in our lives. When we face a transition, such as retirement, we may not have an immediate vision or a known path as to exactly how our lives will pan out during the retirement. This can lead us to experience exaggerated distorted or unpleasant thoughts and feelings about this stage of our lives. These tend to be negative and reflect our fears about how and why we might not cope. They range from mild apprehension such as "I'm not sure that I will cope very well with not having a job to go to", to extreme fears, such as "Life will unbearable if I am no longer the boss". These thoughts, known as "thinking traps" or "thinking errors", may lead us to feel negatively and also act in ways that reflect these negative thoughts rather than what we would normally do. Consider the following example.

> Ben had two months to go before he would retire from his job as head of the marketing department for a big telephone company. For the past four months, he had been gradually handing over his managerial duties to the new staff member who would take over Ben's position. During this time fewer demands were put on Ben by colleagues and clients as they would often direct their queries to the new manager. Ben thought he was "easily replaced and therefore insignificant at work", that people "preferred the new manager" and that colleagues had "lost respect" for him. He felt useless, lonely and insecure. Having always been a sociable person who would often join colleagues for lunch or even the odd drink after work, Ben gradually began to avoid going to the work canteen and he declined invitations to work events. He became

increasingly withdrawn and silent at work. When he finally shared his thoughts and feelings with a long-term colleague of his, Ben was surprised to hear that people in the office were actually sad to see him go. They had thought that by placing less demand on Ben they would allow him to make the most of his last six months at work and enjoy the rest of his career. His department was planning a farewell party to honour Ben's 25 years with the company.

As we have seen, negative thoughts, thinking errors and thinking traps may dent our confidence, lower our mood and make us feel hopeless, vulnerable, depressed and even out of control. We explore these, and give strategies for coping with the resulting fear, worry and anxiety, in Chapter 4.

Fear of change

With retirement, the main fear is that of change. We are talking about a major life change here, with the transition from work to post-work. Fear of the unknown and heightened anxiety about not being in control are also often expressed by people approaching retirement. Life is fragile and vulnerable and none of us – despite our best efforts – has complete control of it. Even though none of us are ever in total control, we can all learn to be in command of our thoughts and feelings. Consider the following case example.

Anna was in charge of a school that she had worked at for thirty years. She had known many of her colleagues for years and really enjoyed working both with them, and the children. Anna had been feeling positive about retirement as she had been looking forward to spending more time with her grandchildren, having more time to study foreign languages, which had always been a hobby of hers, and to be able to go on holiday in "term-time"!

However, as the time drew nearer Anna found herself being unable to sleep at night and started to feel quite panicky, and had her first ever panic attack. She did not know why she was feeling so anxious and felt embarrassed to tell her family and friends about her sleepless nights and feelings of anxiety, as she had always been someone who everyone else viewed as strong and capable. Eventually, Anna decided to tell her husband she had been feeling anxious but did not know why. He said he had felt similarly panicky when he retired from his job, as a GP, five years earlier.

Anna said she had not initially thought her anxiety was linked to her impending retirement but after thinking about it she realised that she was nervous about suddenly being at home all the time. Anna was worried that she and her husband might have difficulty adjusting to spending so much time together when they were both used to their independent routines. Her husband reassured her that he had become busier than ever since retiring, that he still valued both his independence and hers, and that things wouldn't change as much as she feared.

Anna realised that another worry was about not feeling needed as much, as she was used to giving support to both teachers and pupils. Anna decided she wanted to volunteer for a local counselling organisation for young people and did some in-house training. She enjoyed being placed on their phone-line where she offered support to adolescents, which made her realise that she could be helpful to people in many various ways and retiring had allowed her to discover other skills she had.

How people react to change

At around the time of life changes, people can react in different ways:

- Some may experience increased internal tension. This may have a ripple effect on other relationships.
- Some people become more involved or more detached emotionally.
- Change may give rise to "rigidity" in patterns of relating, or the opposite – being immobilised with fear.
- Great projects may be started and huge life changes initiated.
- Or the individual may seem "stuck" in the process of change, ignore or even deny some important challenges or tasks, and accomplish nothing at all. If becoming stuck occurs, this may give rise to symptomatic behaviour (low mood, irritability, sleep problems, etc.).
- A person may become more worried, anxious or unsettled than usual.

Ask yourself: What is your attitude to change? Are you able to tolerate uncertainty or does the thought of "not knowing" fill you with dread? Think about the last time you experienced a significant change in your life – how did you deal with the transition? Was there anything you did that made it

> easier to deal with the change? What coping strategies, if any, did or did not work for you at that moment in your life?

Psychological techniques to overcome fear

As we have stressed, there are many reasons why people develop fears in the first place. These will often vary from one person to another due to individual differences in bodily reactions, feelings of lacking in control, and thinking styles to name a few. This is why psychologists do not find it effective to treat fears in a "one-size-fits-all" approach. There are psychological techniques you can apply to help you deal with transitions in your life so that you can overcome your fear of change and encourage you to break free from the reinforcing cycle of negative thoughts and emotions. We discuss these further in Chapter 4.

How to avoid overreacting

It is normal from time to time to experience catastrophic thoughts, apprehension, fear and even some panicky feelings in certain situations. We are psychologically "designed" to recognise and react to stressful events and to instinctively mount a fight against the person or animal that we fear will do us harm, or to flee from danger ("fight or flight" reflex). As a species, this is one reason that humans have survived and, indeed, thrived. However, this instinct can be triggered too often or too intensely, perhaps when the threat is real but not quite life-threatening. It is a difficult instinct to override and control but, with some practice, applying countermeasures relating to our thinking patterns and our physical/bodily reactions can help to prevent, stem or curtail the frequency and intensity of some of our reactions, thereby helping us to feel more in control of a situation. This is the basis of cognitive behavioural therapy, which is widely used both within the NHS and also by many therapists and psychologists working independently in private practice (see Chapter 4).

The starting point is to identify the specific thoughts or patterns in a person's thinking which may have a negative impact on his or hers emotional and physical wellbeing. Some of these are highlighted in Chapter 4 where we discuss thinking errors, including all-or-nothing thinking, overgeneralisation, jumping to conclusions and catastrophising, among others. Examples from those we have helped professionally include worries about a loss of a sense of purpose and a fear of being left out of other people's lives and feeling lonely. To help you identify unhelpful ways of anticipating or experiencing your retirement, you may wish to start by reflecting on what might be driving some negative thoughts.

> Ask yourself: Can you think of anything that may be amplifying or causing unhelpful thoughts at the moment? Are there particular stressors in your life that may be relevant (for example, relationship difficulties, health issues, financial constraints, etc.)?

Once you have identified these stressors you can begin to solve some of them. You might, for example, think about acting in some way to strengthen or distance yourself from certain relationships if they are causing your stress and worry. If you are, for example, lacking in purpose you may want to consider implementing positive strategies to counter this, perhaps by taking up new hobbies and pursuing certain interests to counter this fear of a lack of purpose or loneliness. These stressors can cause negative thoughts and by using new strategies to cope with the stressors you are able to reduce these negative thoughts and painful emotions. Adaptive ways of coping can be translated into action points so you begin to work against external stress, unhelpful beliefs and those worries that have instilled fear in the first place. A pattern of negative thinking may be reflected in a tendency towards pessimism about a range of things: "What's the point?!" In which case, you need to examine these patterns and find ways to challenge the tendency by not automatically succumbing to your negative thoughts. Sometimes this is quite straightforward. At other times, it requires the assistance and intervention of a caring friend or, if required, a therapist. Occasionally, such negativism can also reflect an underlying mood problem, in which case it might be time for a visit to your doctor to check this out.

Behavioural remedies to overreacting can include problem solving, reducing avoidance by confronting the situation, seeking support or advice on how to move forward in your life, being motivated to make a start on overcoming the overreaction and assessing what types of tool, support network or changes are needed for you to feel in control of your retirement. For example, if you lack motivation to make changes, you may wish to begin by setting small, achievable goals. This will gradually enhance your motivation to make the positive changes in your life that will help with the retirement process. Research has shown that our motivation to do anything in life is often enhanced by actively "doing" something rather than passively burying our head in the sand. Sometimes this means being brave enough to ask for help, and at other times it may involve trying new things that perhaps you initially thought would not work for you. It is only when we do something different that we can start to create a positive path in our lives. You may take the wrong turn now and again, but by committing to taking the turn in the first place you will be closer to knowing which will be the right one for you. If you are feeling particularly anxious or worried you may want to consider:

- distracting yourself by focusing your attentions elsewhere;
- taking deep breaths so as to lower your heart rate;
- practising mindfulness, yoga or meditation to relax you; or
- increasing your aerobic exercise.

Relaxation training is another way of reducing worry or anxiety. Try clenching your buttocks for five seconds, then relaxing. Or tap your middle finger as fast as you can while humming gently as a way to distract and relax you. You can find many good relaxation techniques online including visual relaxation, progressive muscular relaxation and deep breathing.

It is important to take action: do something different! The remedy to negative thoughts, worry and anxiety is to find different ways to react to them; not to ignore them, keep repeating predictable patterns, or become immobilised with fear. If this happens, it's probably time to seek advice and help from those close to you, perhaps from an ex-colleague with whom you are still friends, or a therapist whose expertise it is to treat these sorts of issues. Modern therapies for stress, worry, anxiety and panicky feelings are usually very effective and, in some cases, measurable progress is made in just a single session. So don't avoid seeking help if it's needed.

Factors that affect "healthy" adjustment

When retirement is combined with poor health and poor finances, we can become weighed down, especially when we are older and can see no way out. A number of factors can affect how healthily we can adjust:

- Being able to retire of your own free will.
- Being able to retire at age 55 or younger.
- Saving towards retirement and being financially independent and debt-free.

- Engaging in "purposeful activity" for more than 5 hours per week.
- Having someone on whom you can rely on for emotional support.
- Having people who you can connect with emotionally.
- Building and maintaining enduring friendships.
- Spending time with your family, especially the youngsters.
- Proactively maintaining or improving health through exercise, mental stimulation, a healthier diet, drinking water, and regular medical checks.
- Stopping or reducing smoking will give you increased life expectancy and better health, whatever your age.
- Adapting your home to suit you, or even moving house.
- Planning ahead for retirement and old age – financial, emotional, practical. According to the Ready for Ageing Alliance, planning for old age is difficult – we tend not to expect to suffer ill health, bereavement or a job loss. A little thinking about how we respond to these challenges can make for a better old age. This includes making a will and funeral arrangements.
- Having fun!

Emotional instability

Emotional instability through retirement may be triggered by the loss of:

- status;
- identity;
- creativity;
- fulfilment;
- productivity and work;
- interest and engagement;
- goals and plans;
- control;
- structure;
- balance in one's life;
- fun, adventure, keeping busy;
- mental and physical stimulation;
- mixing with people and developing social networks;
- income;
- purpose;
- certainty around health and body; and
- bodily esteem.

Some of these need to be maintained or replaced. Consider the following case example.

> Sue and Nadine, both airline industry workers, formalised their five-year relationship by entering into a civil partnership and they both set about saving up enough money so that they would not have to work for a while and thus could enjoy being together while they were relatively young. Things changed, however, when the couple decided to embark on parenthood. Both Sue and Nadine became pregnant by artificial insemination by donor and, within the space of three years, life as they knew it had changed beyond recognition. They were the proud parents of a one- and two-year-old son and daughter.
>
> Sue and Nadine recognised that they did not immediately need to return to work and they had enough funds to keep their family going for at least ten years, which would therefore be halfway through their children's school education. However, in discussion, the couple recognised their goal of having an early retirement had been turned on its head. They felt that they needed to go back to work for two main reasons. The first was an obvious financial one as they were concerned about the medium- and long-term financial implications of bringing up a family.
>
> Furthermore, they also discussed what it would mean to their children when they started school, what would happen if their children or other parents asked what their parents did for a living. They felt it would be good role modelling for them each to have jobs so that their children learned to adjust to parents who had jobs and other interests and commitments. The couple also felt that there would come a time, obviously many years from now, when their children would presumably leave home and, without the work stimulation, this could leave them at a loose end at a stage of life when perhaps they would benefit from, or need, the mental stimulation.

> **Ask yourself:** What can you start doing now to maintain your emotional stability in the future?

What family behaviour have we inherited and how will this impact on our retirement? Sometimes these can be negative, sometimes positive. We need to be aware what is driving our emotions and identify these scripts or schemas, as they can be problematic. Think about this and discuss it with your partner.

> Ask yourself: What family scripts have you been following? For example, are there particular rules or assumptions about diet, health and wellbeing in your family? What about communication and views on relationships? Can you identify how individual members within the family may hold similar (or different) outlooks on life?

Consider another case example ...

> Bernice, a senior A&E nurse, had been feeling excited and positive for a number of months about her impending retirement at the end of the year. She had put a big red ring round the date on her calendar at home but as the months passed she started to feel growing apprehension. She had lived with her twin sister Rebecca since their parents had died a number of years before and also had a younger brother, Tom, who had a young family and lived in America. Bernice had not seen her brother for a number of years due to her work commitments. She had often talked about visiting him, but the time had never been right. Rebecca, a retired art teacher, talked endlessly about how wonderful retirement was, filling every minute with meeting friends or enjoying different hobbies.
> Rebecca kept trying to make plans for Bernice, who was starting to feel increasingly out of control – as if the very foundation and structure of her life was falling apart. She was beginning to wake up at night with palpitations and found herself sweating and restless. She felt unable to approach her sister and express her fears to her as Rebecca was so positive; Bernice felt "silly" and embarrassed about her feelings. The truth was she was starting to feel more and more anxious and frightened about her retirement. She found herself getting tearful on the ward and felt vulnerable and alone. In some ways, she described feeling the same as when she was a little girl being left at the school gates for the first time.
> Bernice decided to seek out her close work colleague, Donald, to express how she was feeling. Donald was extremely helpful and kind, giving her the confidence to reach out to others and express her concerns. She talked to a neighbour who had retired the year before and who she remembered had taken some time to adapt. By sharing her feelings and being open to suggestions she began to

think creatively about retirement. She started to look at it as a new and exciting adventure. Bernice had dedicated her entire professional life to caring for others and, having worked in A&E with a number of patients who had been victims of crime, she decided that she had a lot to offer in working with Victim Support. She took on two cases while she was still working, enjoying this experience immensely and thus giving herself options for when she retired. Donald suggested that she reduce her working week by a day, which gave her an opportunity to gradually adapt and plan how to structure her future. Bernice also felt more confident to talk to her sister because she was now carving out her own life which was separate from Rebecca's. She started to make concrete plans to visit her brother in America – something she had never had the time to do before.

Bernice started to meet friends, and getting used to a slower pace of life – but one which had the hope and potential of being just as fulfilling in a new way. Once she adapted her thinking she began to have more restful nights, feel more in charge of her life and empowered to embrace the future with new-found optimism. She became less tearful and was able to enjoy the last few months of her work. She would remain in contact with work colleagues, meaning she would be able to keep up to date with what was happening. As she discovered a new reality for herself, she also discovered aspects of herself that she had not considered before. She was able to accept that her way was different to that of her sister, and realised that this difference could bring a new and exciting richness to their relationship.

The subject of "retirement" is in fact a good prompt to address a whole raft of psychological issues. Not least of these are goals and expectations. Relationships are important when setting goals for the future. Talk about your personal, couple and family goals for retirement with your partner. Remember it is healthy to have both individual and separate goals. Make sure there is communication and flexibility within these goals, and revisit them regularly. Also ensure you have discussed and decided upon your expectations of the future, with regard to what you hope to attain and the legacy you want to leave, both tangible and intangible.

How we think about things is a fascinating subject, and we delve deeper into this in the next chapter.

Chapter 3

The maturing brain

So, why do we think the thoughts outlined in the previous chapter? Here's what is going on in the brain as we age.

What happens to the mature mind?

Growing older causes physiological and mental changes. Some are due to family or genetic patterns of ageing; others are down to your lifestyle choices (fortunately, we can control the latter).

Normal ageing involves changes to:

- bones – throughout adult hood your bones are demineralising, causing risk of osteoporosis;
- ears – you will experience high-frequency hearing loss and will find changes in tone less clear;
- eyes – vision for reading, visual sharpness and night vision will decline, and glare will become more of a problem;
- fingernails – the growth will slow down;
- hair – will become greyer, and scalp, pubic and armpit hair will gradually thin;
- height – compression of the spine and changes in posture will mean you become shorter;
- metabolism – will slow, and you will accumulate more body fat rather than muscle mass;
- skin – will become less elastic, drier and more wrinkled;
- sleep – you will sleep less and not as deeply, and experience more interrupted sleep and an earlier awakening;
- and, of course, the brain ...

Mental processing as we age

The brain is basically a collection of nerve cells – neurons – which make multiple connections with other nerve cells. That network of connections enables us to process information, store memories, reason, solve problems, feel emotions and control our bodies. Neuroscientists call these cognitive tasks. Neurons extend from the brain, into our spinal cord and most of the rest of our body to collect information and deliver commands – but it's the brain that acts as the central hub. The network of connections starts to form before birth and continues to develop rapidly into our early twenties. In healthy adults, the rate at which new connections are created slows down but never completely stops. Some connections become unconscious or automatic pathways – pulling back from painful stimuli, for example.

Developing long-term memory and skills such as walking or riding a bicycle rely on rehearsal and repetition to develop robust and easily accessed connections in our brain. It's like making a well-worn track through a field by walking the same route often. The more connections we make in specific parts of the brain, the larger volume that part will take up. A structure called the hippocampus is one of the main parts of the brain that stores long term memories. Studies have shown that it increases in size for London taxi drivers who successfully study "The Knowledge" and effectively memorise a map of London. Interestingly, when these taxi drivers retire and stop actively using this information, it seems that their hippocampus often reduces to a more average size. So there is some evidence for "use it or lose it" (i.e. using our brains helps to maintain some physical structures within them and the associated functions).

Modern research suggests that some parts of most healthy adult brains decrease in size slightly as we get older. This is particularly likely to happen to the hippocampus and a structure called the prefrontal cortex, which plays a significant role in planning and complex tasks such as decision making. Connections between neurons can be disrupted by chemical and physical changes associated with ageing. All of these can result in sometimes barely noticeable changes in the way our brain functions. It may become more difficult to learn new things or retrieve memorised information, particularly if that information is not used often. In many cognitive tasks such as learning and memorising, however, recent studies have shown that people in their seventies or eighties will perform just as well as people in their twenties if given enough time. So it may take more time to learn new things, but it can be done just as well!

On a more positive note, neuroscientists have recently shown that, as we age, our brains may adapt to use alternative ways of doing cognitive tasks such as learning or memorising. There isn't a complete explanation, yet, as to how and why this happens. It seems to be the case that, if one structure in our brains becomes slightly less active or even damaged, other regions of the brain may take over or assist in completing cognitive tasks. This is what is meant when the brain is called "plastic": It is a flexible structure that, in the right circumstances can adapt how different structures are used to complete important tasks. Although it's not completely understood in adults yet, it may be that it is possible to take action to sustain good brain function into old age. It is also the reason that it is sometimes possible for adults to recover from the damage caused by a stroke. What we know about helping to keep our brains healthy and functioning well at the moment is outlined in the following section.

Some physical diseases increase the rate at which our brains change, or cause damage beyond the brain's plastic ability to adapt. Dementia, Alzheimer's disease, stroke and physical injury are the most common causes. The results can range from minor problems that may require some lifestyle adaptations or intermittent care to significant impairment needing full time specialist care. This book is not the place to explore those in great detail but we have included some information on dementia in the following sections.

Dementia

Dementia is a term used to describe a set of symptoms caused by a gradual loss of brain function. These include memory loss, difficulties with communication and reasoning, and mood changes. They can be caused by a wide range of physical conditions including vascular disease and Alzheimer's disease. These symptoms can have other causes. For example, untreated infections can cause memory loss and confusion. Careful assessment and diagnosis of any symptoms like these is crucial to the best outcome so our advice is always talk to your GP or healthcare professional if you're concerned and don't jump to conclusions.

The question most people ask is "can dementia be prevented?" At the moment, it isn't possible to guarantee that anything will completely prevent dementia. Again, a healthy lifestyle with attention to diet, exercise and your physical health is the best advice available. Excessive use of alcohol and smoking do increase the risk of developing dementia in older age.

Dementia is an experience that will vary significantly from one person to another. It's currently a frequent topic in the media and something that can, understandably, seem very frightening. Here are some helpful approaches:

1 If you have seen close friends or family members struggle with dementia or cared for someone with advanced symptoms, it may become something that creates significant and frequent anxiety as you get older. That can, unfortunately, have an adverse effect on your own wellbeing. If you become anxious imagining that you will have a very similar difficult experience to someone you know, remember that everyone's individual experience is very different. The aspects of their experience that concern you the most may not happen to you.
2 If you find yourself worrying, ask yourself if it's (a) realistic and (b) useful to worry about your health right now. If your concerns are realistic and there is something you or someone else should or can do to help (for example, make an appointment to see your GP) then make a plan to do that and try to distract yourself when you don't need to be following that plan. If it's not realistic or helpful to focus on your concerns right now, again find something that distracts you. The activities we describe next can be useful in this.
3 If you are worried that you have dementia or if you become so anxious that it's affecting your health or wellbeing, ask your GP for advice and possibly professional help. There is a range of practical and therapeutic techniques that can help you and your family deal with dementia.
4 Anxiety can be experienced over a prolonged period of time. Are you concerned you might be becoming one of your GP's "frequent fliers"? If so, agree with them what symptoms you should look for and when to make another appointment.

If you want to know more about dementia, there are some well-written articles on the NHS Choices, Alzheimer's Research UK and Dementia UK websites (see Resources).

Keeping your brain fit

The first thing to say is that aiming for the best possible physical health is the foremost thing you can do to help your brain function as well as possible. A sensible diet, regular exercise (both weight bearing and cardiovascular or aerobic) and keeping an eye on your weight, cholesterol and blood pressure promote good blood supply to the brain and reduce the risk of damage from disease. There is lots of conflicting advice about supplements and "superfoods" for brain health. There is, however, very little evidence to prove their benefit and some supplements can be very expensive to take in the long term. The current NHS advice is that, if you're eating a balanced diet, they're probably not beneficial, but do talk to your GP or pharmacist if you think you might need a supplement (see also Chapter 8).

We're often asked if there's a benefit from keeping mentally active, for example by doing crosswords or puzzles. The answer is "probably"! An increasing amount of research suggests that adults who consistently engage in intellectually stimulating activities from their sixties onwards who do not have or develop disease or injury are better at cognitive tasks in their seventies and eighties. This doesn't mean you should feel guilty if you don't enjoy doing the crossword daily though. What's most likely to be effective for you is something that uses the cognitive skills which are important to you and that you enjoy doing. Also remember that, although it is probably true that mentally stimulating activities will help keep your brain functioning well, your genetic makeup, environment, physical health, lifestyle and experience will all play their part. We can control some, but not all, of the factors that keep our brains functioning well.

Most evidence about what works comes from studies that use formal "brain training" activities such as computer-based memory practice sessions or attention training. These aren't necessarily easy to replicate at home and they may not be activities that you find sufficiently interesting or engaging to use regularly. You're aiming for tasks that involve planning, concentration, decision making and learning, which you actually want to do for a few minutes on most days. The oft-quoted crossword puzzle, sudoku or number puzzles do fit that description for some.

Intellectually stimulating activities that will keep your brain active can include:

- learning something new;
- planning and reading around hobbies;
- using more than one language regularly;
- engaging in creative activities such as art, writing, knitting or dressmaking;

- visiting the theatre or participating in a drama group;
- undertaking Internet-based research (an academic subject, current affairs or finding the best price for a major purchase); and
- being socially active (such as seeing friends and family, talking to neighbours or visiting public areas where you can be around people).

The list is potentially endless; what's important is that it's meaningful and engaging for you and fits with your life. Trawling through seed catalogues and planning your garden or allotment is an intellectual activity. So are some computer games and smartphone apps!

Common "purposeful" activities

If all that seems a bit lightweight, here are some ideas for you that involve more of a purpose:

- Get involved in social, voluntary, or activity based groups – become a school governor or charity fundraiser if that appeals.
- Set up your own business.
- Take further education classes (there is a huge range out there, from informal talks to degree courses and beyond).
- Undertake consultancy work.
- Teach others – be a teacher, trainer, coach or mentor.
- Take up a non-executive directorship.
- Get involved in charity work.
- Become the secretary or join the committee of a local club, church, etc.
- Care for others, such as elderly parents or grandchildren.
- Join or set up an alumni group from your last job/employer.
- Use or build on your existing skills by not being afraid to commit to regular activities.

If you're not sure what you can do, speak to others in order to get ideas.

Giving back

Volunteering

The ILC, with the Commission on the Voluntary Sector and Ageing, published a report in 2014 titled *A Better Offer*, looking at the future of volunteering in an ageing society. Charities are reliant on volunteering, but their core retiree helpers are growing older, and younger people are under pressure to work longer and care for their families, so reducing the time available to volunteer. Volunteering by older people was valued at £24 billion a year, with around 23 million people in England volunteering in 2012, more than half of them at least once a month.

So charities are dependent on our help. But if we volunteer, we may want to give our help in more modern ways. As the report asks, "Will volunteers with long, often challenging careers behind them settle for licking envelopes and setting out chairs, or will they expect and demand more? Will they willingly help run services for free which were traditionally provided by the state? Will charities adapt to attract a retiring generation which is more confident and tech-savvy than ever before?" We watch with interest how the charities are responding to this challenge.

We want to remind you that there are huge benefits to your health in volunteering, so it is always worth considering if you have the time. And there is a place in your new post-retirement portfolio career for the variety, social interaction and other rewards that volunteering brings.

The ILC report lists these other rewards as:

- The buzz – a physical and emotional well-being and sense of satisfaction.
- Structure and routine – these are often missing in retirees' lives, and helping a charity can help in periods of transition like retirement, divorce and bereavement.
- Personal development – learning new skills and giving back their accumulated experience and knowledge.

In addition, as shown in a meta-analysis by the Rotman Research Institute in Toronto (published in *Psychological Bulletin*) of 73 studies exploring volunteering in the over fifties, additional benefits are: reduced symptoms of depression, better overall health and greater longevity. They identify the optimal amount of time to volunteer as between two and three hours a week.

A five-year multi-institutional study by Michael Poulin and colleagues into altruism (published in the *American Journal of Public Health*) discovered that giving and being unselfish not only helps others, but can also protect the health and prolong the lives of the altruistic. As Poulin says, "giving assistance to others may offer health benefits to the giver by buffering the negative effects of stress". He concludes:

These findings go beyond past analyses to indicate that the health benefits of helping behaviour derive specifically from stress-buffering processes, and provide important guidance for understanding why helping behaviour specifically may promote health and, potentially, for how social processes in general may influence health.

Here are just a few national organisations that rely on volunteers:

- The National Trust (www.nationaltrust.org.uk), whose website declares "It's the skills, passion and time of our volunteers that make our places special".
- The Retired and Senior Volunteering Programme (RSVP) is the only specialist UK-wide organisations for over-50s (csv-rsvp.org.uk).
- The Blue Cross (www.bluecross.org.uk) rely on volunteers for many of their activities.
- Maggie's Centres are buildings in the grounds of hospitals, specially designed for those diagnosed with cancer and their families and friends. Practical, emotional and social support is offered.

Contact Volunteering.org.uk (020 7713 6161) to find out about volunteering opportunities in your area. Also, www.gov.uk has lots of useful information, as does www.totaljobs.com.

Become a trustee

Becoming the trustee of a charity can be extremely worthwhile. See www.trusteenet.org.uk or www.smallcharities.org.uk. Or you could set up a charity yourself, if you have a cause close to your heart.

Mentoring

Mentoring others can be very satisfying. Passing on your skills and knowledge, and the benefit of your experience, is empowering and self-affirming. Here are some ideas:

- Barnardo's and other charities use retired or semi-retired executives to mentor senior staff.
- The Prince's Initiative for Mature Enterprise (PRIME) has mentoring schemes matching experienced professionals to aspiring entrepreneurs aged 50+.
- Most schools welcome people with a few spare hours per week to listen to children read or provide one-on-one support to a disadvantaged

child, such as a recent immigrant. Simply approach the head teacher to enquire about the possibilities available. You will require a DBS check, as with any position involving contact with children.

The following case example illustrates the benefits of mentoring.

Roger, a senior partner in a law firm, was nervous in his approach to retirement and had continued to postpone it for a number of years. While his wife, children and friends encouraged him to take his much-deserved retirement, Roger found that he was resisting. Through a conversation with an old friend he identified that, although he was concerned about losing a number of things when leaving work (e.g. daily routine and structure, intellectual challenge, identity as a successful lawyer), he was most concerned about no longer having contact with his younger colleagues.

Roger had always taken a lot of joy in working with and mentoring the younger members of his team and watching them develop. He also enjoyed the energy of younger people. Now that his own children were grown up he was dreading the idea of spending time solely with people from his generation.

Roger's friend told him about a mentoring organisation that his retired sister worked for. Roger was delighted to hear that this type of thing was available, and learned that there were opportunities to mentor young people professionally, and also within schools and other organisations.

In preparation for his retirement, Roger attended training to be a mentor and signed up to mentor four young professionals in need of guidance in their career paths. By the time he retired he was already meeting each of his mentees on a monthly basis. Although retirement was a huge adjustment for Roger, he found that by identifying the aspects he would miss most about work he was able to start planning for them and look to replace them with other things. Mentoring was not the same as working every day with younger colleagues, but Roger found it to be extremely fulfilling.

Join an altruistic society, or become a fundraiser

There are many organisations that exist to raise funds for others less fortunate, known as service clubs, for example:

- The Rotary Club
- The Soroptimists

- The Round Table
- The Lions.

This sort of fundraising centres on social activities for members, and can be very rewarding.

And remember that all charities welcome fundraisers and sponsors. Look at local ones as well as national and international organisations. For example, Saga has a charitable trust.

Pass on your skills

Share your knowledge with others by becoming a tutor. Your local community college may welcome you as a tutor for short courses or workshops. Or, if sport is your thing, you can help coach local teams. Training on teaching and coaching is available.

Local radio shows are always looking for people to interview with interesting and unusual experiences, skills or hobbies (see www.radio-now.co.uk). Try your hospital radio too (see www.hbauk.co.uk). Or you could set yourself up as a private tutor, to schoolchildren or adults, in your area of expertise. There will be something you have experience of that will be of value to others - woodworking, helping young mums, business, art, literacy, gardening, French language or even psychology. Reed have a clear explanation of how to go about it (https://www.reed.co.uk/career-advice/how-to-become-a-tutor/).

The power of play

Grandparents, and increasingly great-grandparents, are actively involved in the lives of their young relatives, as the children's parents have to work. This can be extremely beneficial to all concerned, as long as safeguards are put in place to ensure the older members do not become exhausted or feel used. Of course, not everyone has children, grandchildren or great-grandchildren of their own, but one of the most beneficial aspects of childcare can be replicated without children at all! It's playtime!

Adults are not supposed to play, unless it is in a competitive way as in many sports, but play or playfulness is definitely good for us, although it is hard to find the time. One psychiatrist, Stuart Brown, has studied the power of play in a number of different categories of people, including business people, artists, prisoners and Nobel Prize winners. In particular, he found that playing together helps couples connect emotionally and could act as a healing tool.

Play is pleasurable, lacking in purpose and fun! What constitutes play varies for everyone but can include team or individual sports, arts and crafts, exercise, hobbies like antique collecting or gardening, restoration projects and so on. Really, it's whatever boosts your happiness.

If this feels like an alien concept to you, don't worry. Just think about what you did as a child that you enjoyed. Did you prefer to be alone or with others when you did it? How could you recreate that today?

Other tips are to surround yourself with playful people, and be prepared to act spontaneously. And if you can spend time with children then you will benefit from experiencing the magic of play through their eyes.

Even Confucius was a fan of play, believing that it's better to play than do nothing. So, don't be idle – be playful. And bear in mind C. S. Lewis's comment that "some day you will be old enough to start reading fairy tales again".

Consider the following case example.

> Stephen, a pilot, had wanted to fly from his earliest memories. He joined the air cadets as soon as he could and went on to a successful career in the Royal Air Force before joining a civilian airline. He loved every part of his job but especially the skill and mastery involved in flying large jet aircraft all over the world. He dreaded retirement because he didn't want to stop flying. (Although he would be able to continue flying light aircraft, he didn't get nearly the same level of fulfilment from that.)
>
> When Stephen was 53, two years before he was due to retire and seven years before he had to, he was offered a voluntary early retirement package. This was so generous that he would be financially rewarded for retiring early. After much soul searching, Stephen decided to take the package. He found very quickly that he missed flying and started to search for another job. It's always been difficult for older pilots to find new flying jobs because it's expensive to train even experienced pilots when they join a new airline. Stephen expanded his search to look worldwide and eventually took a contract for two years in Dubai.
>
> Stephen's wife, Mary, was still working and he initially moved to Dubai without her. They both hated being apart, so Mary retired early and moved to Dubai to join him. At the end of the two years, Stephen promised Mary that he would take her round the world in style before they returned home.
>
> They got as far as their first stop, Singapore, visiting friends, when Stephen received a call asking if he'd like to take a short contract in Italy. He accepted and left almost immediately to start

his training with the new airline, leaving Mary to cancel their travel plans and follow him.

They spent a very happy 18 months in Italy and returned to the UK when Stephen was 57. He still didn't feel ready to stop flying and joined a UK Airline that was fairly new and actively recruiting experienced pilots. He eventually retired for the final time just before his sixtieth birthday.

Both Stephen and Mary struggled for a while when Stephen finally retired. Mary wasn't used to having him at home so much and Stephen missed flying. By that stage, his son was also working as an airline pilot and Stephen would constantly ask for details of his son's flights.

When the family got together for Christmas the year after Stephen retired, they talked about the couple's plans. The conversation led both Mary and Stephen to realise that they could choose to focus on what they couldn't do any more, or upon new challenges. They both decided to learn to play golf, even though the family teased them about this being a retirement cliché! While not for everyone, for them golf provided time together, something they both enjoyed, structure to their week, and exercise. They also made time to keep up with their own friends and interests. Stephen particularly enjoyed becoming the head of the local Neighbourhood Watch team, thriving on making a contribution to the community and the feeling of responsibility that brought him.

Two years after retiring, Stephen brought the family teasing to a halt by describing their recipe for a good life after work comes to an end: Find some structure and activities that are important to you and share some of them with the people you love.

Use it or lose it

So, the more you challenge your brain, the stronger it becomes. It will continue to grow new brain cells and make new connections. Plan these regular activities to boost your brain:

- undertake mental exercise;
- engage in physical exercise, especially aerobic;
- challenge yourself;
- work towards mastering skills;
- develop social networks;
- give back; and
- play.

More tips for improving your mental health

- Get out and about. Try to get out of the house every day, even just for a short walk. Keep busy and spread out appointments and events across the week so you always have something to do.
- Have a clear out. If you are divorced or widowed, you may wish to make the effort to move things around in your home to suit you – altering your environment is good for you. Change of this nature can help you to "reclaim" your home space and project your wishes and feelings onto your living environment. These physical and symbolic changes can help to "re-set" some of your feelings.
- Change your routines. This might sound odd but sleeping on the other side of the bed, sitting at a different place at the table, moving your armchair or the television, shopping at another supermarket and buying and eating new foods all add novelty and excitement to your life, which is good for your mental health.
- Treat yourself. Boost your self-esteem with a haircut, some new make-up or clothes or a new pair of glasses. Your confidence will thank you for it and compliments from others are always wonderful.

> Ask yourself: How can you care for yourself to maintain or build a healthy self-esteem.

In the next chapter we look further at the challenging feelings and behaviours that you might experience at this time of your life, and give you strategies to help you deal with them.

Chapter 4

Psychological approaches to challenging feelings and behaviours

The transition from working life to retirement, like any other significant lifespan changes, may pose significant practical and psychological challenges. The general trend for greater longevity means that a concern for soon to be retirees is the provision of quality and peace of mind for the years ahead. Retirement may represent a welcome relief from the pressures and stress of the work place, but it is also the start of a new unknown with many challenges. Ensuring ongoing financial security, filling the void previously filled by employment, creating structure, engaging meaningfully with life, optimising life satisfaction, contending with health issues and dealing with the process of ageing and even death may be just some of the challenges that lay ahead. There are any number of circumstances and difficult life events that can be attached to the period of retirement. The psychological impact of facing some of these challenges may include:

- increased fear, worry and anxiety;
- loss, grief and bereavement;
- low mood;
- increased negative thoughts;
- sleep problems; and
- addictions and alcohol dependency.

Even if retirement is well thought through and planned for, none of us are immune from the existential challenges that life can suddenly present us with. The focus of this chapter is to consider some of the psychological, emotional and behavioural challenges that may be involved in this transitional period, and to provide some constructive ways for addressing these based on a cognitive and behavioural psychological approach.

Fear, worry and anxiety: thinking errors

As we mentioned in Chapter 2, fear is a natural human response and, although facing our fears can be incredibly challenging at times, not addressing them can lead to us becoming overwhelmed with worry. Worry can have an increasingly negative impact on our psychological wellbeing. Fears and concerns about retirement will vary among individuals. One person may tend to worry about how they will manage financially post retirement; for another, fear of isolation may be the biggest cause for concern.

Worry is usually triggered in relation to a situation which we perceive may have undesirable outcomes. Problematic situations are likely to trigger unpleasant thoughts. Often these thoughts will occur in relation to a current situation that we are facing in our lives; however, we may also find ourselves worrying about a future event or situation. Worry may vary from individual to individual and is largely dependent on the way we view things. We all hold different expectations and beliefs about situations. Those individuals who tend to take a negative view of life and who expect the worst will often be those who tend to worry the most. Some individuals have the tendency to catastrophise and this process often makes worry feel out of control, creating anxiety. If the problem causing the worry is dealt with effectively then the worry will naturally subside; however, if the problem remains unresolved, it is possible that the worry will continue to escalate, fuelling anxiety. There are several factors that are therefore important for addressing worry:

- recognising unhelpful negative thoughts;
- restructuring negative thoughts;
- problem solving; and
- talking through our worries and concerns with others.

Anxiety is often associated with uncertainty. It is a completely normal response to any difficult or challenging circumstance and can be triggered by venturing into the unknown. It is understandable that any individual facing a significant transition in life such as retirement may experience some anxiety. It will require adjustment to impending changes and elements of uncertainty in regard to how the next chapter in your life will unfold.

Strategies for coping with fear, worry and anxiety

Giving reassuring statistics to those who present for treatment with fears and phobias may not help them to overcome their fear. Many people who seek help already know these facts. Instead, psychologists have more recently turned their attention to looking at how to cope with the irrational part of people's fears and devising ways in which those feared situations can be more positively managed. There are several ways in which targeted psychological therapy can help you to overcome fear, worry and anxiety, and we recommend this if your fears are getting in the way of things for you.

For example, anxiety may be best understood by thinking about it in the context of the cognitive and behavioural psychological model. Cognitive behavioural therapy (CBT) is a modern, practical and evidence-based model. The model suggests that in any given situation there are four aspects that are going on that dictate how you experience that situation:

1   Thoughts. This refers to your mental activity or what is going on in your mind. It is sometimes referred to as cognition. This might include images, memories, ideas, beliefs, judgements, worries and fantasies.
2   Feelings. This refers to your emotional experience or mood. Usually we can name our feelings using one word. For example, "anxious", "sad", "angry", "jealous", "happy", "frustrated".
3   Behaviour. This refers to what you are doing. For example, going for a walk, talking to a friend, mowing the lawn or making a coffee.
4   Body. This relates to how you are feeling physically. What is your physiological experience? For example, nauseous, headache, accelerated heartbeat, tingling sensation in fingers.

These four components are interconnected and all affect each other. For this reason, you can develop patterns and cycles that can be self-perpetuating. Some of these patterns can be very unhelpful and can contribute to negative experiences and suffering, such as anxiety and low mood. The good news is that if you can make a change to one part of entry to the cycle, then the whole cycle can change. When you start to understand the cycles you tend to get stuck in, you can plan how to change them and develop new and more helpful and adaptive patterns to reduce your overall experience of suffering.

When you are faced with uncertainty it may trigger anxious exaggerated, unpleasant and inaccurate or distorted thoughts. These thoughts may reflect your concerns about how you are going to manage and what might prevent you from coping satisfactorily. They may vary in extremes from "I wonder whether my new projects will generate the income I'd like to achieve" to "managing my expenses is going to be a total struggle". Inevitably, such thoughts can have a detrimental impact on your confidence levels, anxiety and mood, and generally contribute to a feeling of not being in control of your life. Psychologists have recognised that the way in which we think about a situation can have a powerful effect on the way we feel. A number of common thinking styles that drive our negative emotions have been identified by David Burns, an eminent psychologist at Stanford University in the USA, who published the classic book *Feeling Good* in 1980. His ideas focused on how mood affects our thoughts and behaviour and how best to challenge negative mood through cognitive therapy by challenging unhelpful behaviours and thoughts.:

1 All or nothing thinking or black and white thinking: a tendency to think in absolute terms or in extreme, mostly negative, ways. For example, "I'm no good to anyone now that I'm out of work, I'm pretty useless", or "I could never be happy if I weren't working." This discounts the fact that you are actually still highly valued by many people including family, friends and ex-colleagues, even though the validation is no longer derived from the professional context now that you have retired.
2 Over-generalisation: taking an individual case and making it apply in general terms, usually false ones. For example, "I didn't make a valuable enough contribution to the charity fundraiser", or the fact that your father simply gave up when he retired, and died shortly afterwards. With regard to the first example: So, you didn't reach your target, but it doesn't mean that your contribution was not worthy, valued and appreciated. The second example discounts other relevant information such as the fact that you know other people who enjoy being retired.
3 Mental filter: focusing on negative thoughts or upsetting experiences rather than those that paint a different picture. Important information tends to be ignored or discounted. For example, "The loss of my working income is going to be an issue in providing for the future." The reality is that even though the usual monthly salary that you have been used to is not going to be generated, you do have other sources of income that should see you in good stead and allow you to lead a comfortable life in retirement. Also, a large number of people manage perfectly well on small pensions.
4 Disqualifying the positive: discounting positive experiences as you do not want to validate them and being unable to shift a pessimistic view of life to one of greater optimism. For example, "Our marriage has been a successful union; however, now that I'm

retiring and that there are going to be changes, it is bound to cause friction." Even though historically the relationship has proved to be a solid one, you still tend to predict the future of the relationship negatively. Another example: "Even though we have saved for our pension pot, we probably won't live long enough to spend it" – a common negative view, usually with no basis in fact at all!

5 Jumping to conclusions or mind reading: assuming the worst will happen without having evidence to support that assumption. For example, "The ache that I have recently been aware of in my knee is the sign of my health going downhill. It must be something bad or sinister." You tend to speculate about things, drawing catastrophic conclusions without even having visited the GP to find out what the ache is about. Or "I could have a panic attack and possibly die" in spite of the fact that the two events are hardly linked and you have never previously suffered a panic attack.

6 Catastrophising: interpreting characteristics of a person or aspects of a situation in a negative, exaggerated way. For example, "We're simply not going to be able to afford to pay the bills and will have to move." Or "By the time I retire pension pots will be taxed so heavily it's not worth saving for the future at all." You tend to foreclose on the absolutely worst case scenario even though this is a very unlikely outcome.

7 Emotional reasoning: making decisions based on the way you feel rather than on the facts or realities. For example, "I'm feeling so anxious I know I won't possibly pass this test." You base your predictions on what is going to happen on the way that you feel, rather than other relative factors such as "I've worked really hard for this, my practice tests have all gone well". Another example: "I feel very anxious. My heart is pounding and I feel faint. Something bad is going to happen on this trip; I just know it."

8 "Should", "must", "ought" and "have to": distorted thinking that fixates on rigid rules, making you inflexible in your approach to life. For example, "I must be able to continue to provide for the children and the grandchildren; I have to find an extra source of income." Or "I should be able to cope with this. I shouldn't have any unpleasant feelings. It must be because the pills aren't working. I have to stay indoors from now on." The fixed rules that you set for yourself create unnecessary pressure and stress. (A famous therapist called Albert Ellis slightly irreverently termed this tendency "musterbation".)

9 Labelling or mislabelling: labelling is putting a (usually negative) label on someone or yourself based on just one characteristic or

personality trait; mislabelling is the tendency to put a negative spin to someone. For example, "The reason why she left her husband for a same-sex partner is because he was sexually unattractive." You tend to explain this by drawing a negative conclusion about the man's sexual attractiveness rather than thinking about the woman's sexuality. Here it is similar to over-generalisation: "It was a plane load of frightened passengers", rather than "some passengers got worried when they were told that the flight would need to divert to another airport because of bad weather at our destination".

10 Personalisation and blame: exaggerating causation when the facts don't necessarily support your interpretation. For example, "My next-door neighbour didn't say hello to me in the garden today, I must have done something to upset her." In fact, the neighbour had just received some sad news and was too upset to communicate with anyone. Or "All my toasters stop working sooner or later; it must be me", when in fact the wiring of the socket was faulty.

> Ask yourself: Do you tend to react in any of these ways? Can you identify the specific thinking errors that you tend to use the most? How could you change your thinking errors?

Worrying may sometimes reach frightening proportions, leaving you feeling vulnerable. This can lead to a panic attack. The experience of a panic attack only reinforces the sense of dread in addition to the unpleasant physical signs, thoughts and feelings associated with anxiety and panic. This is called secondary anxiety, when we develop a fear of fear itself. Many people who have a fear also have a fear of the physical and emotional effects of being fearful, which will often cause extreme anxiety or even panic and an avoidance of things or situations in the future because of how unpleasant the thought of the anxiety itself is for the person.

Cognitive behavioural therapy

CBT is an intuitive approach to being stuck. Stress gets locked into predicable patterns. With CBT you can look at what is driving a behaviour and maintaining the cycle, and then change and disrupt the predictable cycle. Think about the following case example.

> Nick is due to retire imminently. While he is fairly relieved at leaving his demanding job behind, he is also worried about the loss

of this long-time job and is especially nervous about his finances. He wonders whether he will be able to manage his bills and expenses adequately. He also has recently experienced some minor health problems and worries about his health deteriorating although there is no evidence to suggest that this will be the case. He wonders about what he is going to do with the extra time that he will have on his hands and whether life will become stagnant. Unfortunately, Nick tends to focus on the worst-case scenarios. This type of thinking elicits feelings of anxiety and nervousness about his retirement. When he finds himself thinking about retirement and the anxiety is triggered, Nick is aware of his elevated heartbeat, muscle tension, headaches and increasing insomnia. Nick becomes fixated with these worrying thoughts about what the future has in store for him and this drives his anxiety.

This example demonstrates the way that the various ports of entry into the cycle are activated. However, intervention in the "thought" port of entry and the "behaviour" port of entry are helpful for impacting on the feelings of anxiety and nervousness and the uncomfortable feelings that Nick experiences in his body. Here's how these work.

Thought activation

Nick should increase his awareness of the thought processes that precipitate his feelings of anxiety and should especially note the inaccurate or unhelpful thoughts. Typically, we tend to be less aware of our thought processes than we are of our feeling states, but we can teach ourselves to shift our attention towards the thoughts. Nick can question whether there is any evidence to support his thinking about his health deteriorating; what have the specialists said to this end? By all accounts they suggest that there is no reason to believe that his health will worsen; in fact, they suggest that it may be improved via changing his diet and engaging in a regular exercise regime. What about the worry about managing his finances? Nick has planned meticulously for his retirement – and indeed has a pension and other investments that suggest he should be able to lead a comfortable life. The evidence suggests that he should be both healthy and financially comfortable during retirement. His thinking style tends to "catastrophise" about his future.

Training ourselves to be more aware of unhelpful thinking processes and learning to challenge them based on the evidence available (i.e. what evidence supports or alternatively does not provide support for the thought in question) can enable us to minimise unwanted experiences of stress and anxiety. The aim of being able to challenge or rationalise unhelpful thoughts is not necessarily to "transform" them into positive thoughts. Instead, it is a helpful way to balance our perceptions by being able to look at a situation, problem or obstacle from various angles. There are, more often than not, multiple ways to interpret a situation.

Let's imagine that you and five friends went to the cinema to watch a film. After the movie the six of you were individually interviewed by a journalist. What would your stories look like? Would they be the exact same narrative or would they be different (with some general similarities of course) based on each person's unique assumptions, experiences and belief systems? The chances are that each interview would vary because each of you have unique life experiences which will shape your individual assumptions and beliefs about the world.

> Ask yourself: Get a pen and a piece of paper. Try to identify up to five unhelpful thoughts or negative thoughts. Can you identify which thinking error they belong to? Next try to challenge each thought by asking the following questions:
>
> 1   How else can I look at this situation?
> 2   How would I advise a friend if he or she was thinking the same as me?
> 3   How would a friend advise me if I shared my thoughts with him or her?

Stress and anxiety management

There are a number of strategies for combatting the symptoms of anxiety and for helping us to relax more effectively. While some people can engage in various activities to help them to relax effectively, for others, learning specific relaxation techniques such as the following can be more helpful:

- Progressive muscle relaxation exercises (a mind/body exercise whereby you focus on contracting and then relaxing different muscle groups to induce an overall sense of relaxation).
- Deep abdominal breathing exercises (a breathing exercise that decreases the release of stress hormones and maximises oxygen in the bloodstream promoting a state of increased relaxation).
- Positive visualisation (the use of visual imagery to conjure up a relaxing/comforting picture using the sensory modalities, e.g. what

you would see, smell, hear if you were sitting on your favourite beach at sunset).
- Mindfulness meditation (the use of sensory stimuli to focus on and accept being fully "in the moment" with the use of enriched awareness).
- Yoga (an ancient Eastern practice which aims to relax and strengthen the body including elements such as posture, breathing, pace, physical alignment and chanting).

Low mood

As with any other life change there is a natural period of adjustment. In the early stages of retirement, it is not uncommon to experience periods of low mood. Retirement may represent a continuation of life but is also a journey towards the unknown. It is a period that determines how one is going to live the rest of their life. Although the theme of this book is "the new retirement", suggesting potential for fulfilment beyond the typical working lifespan, planning ahead, concerns about new endeavours that one plans to embark upon and the uncertainty attached to this may be unsettling. For some this uncertainty may trigger a low mood, which could develop into depression if not addressed. Additionally, for many of us, working life injects meaning and a sense of purpose to our existence, so a radical change to the daily structure and former routine may present us with something of a void.

Typical feelings associated with poor overall mood may be:

- boredom;
- emptiness;
- loneliness; and
- uselessness.

Strategies for dealing with low mood

As with anxiety, it can be useful to think about our low mood in the context of the cycle mapped out earlier in this chapter. How might our thinking be driving uncomfortable emotions, is there anything that we may or may not be doing that contributes to our negative feelings? Consider the following case example.

> George had been employed as an IT consultant for a City bank for the whole of his working life. This has provided him with a good

income to support his family, made him feel valued and respected, and also created a vast social network for him. Although George looked forward to retirement and the idea of being able to relax and enjoy himself more, he found himself feeling as though his "extended vacation" left him more with a sense of emptiness than satisfaction. George started to think of himself as being of little use anymore and viewed his life as being empty and without purpose. As his social life was scaled down without the professional networking that resulted through work, George began to think of himself as having little of interest to offer anybody and began to feel worthless. He subsequently slowly started to withdraw from any social activity and a low mood perpetuated.

Again, awareness of the role of distorted thinking and the ability to recognise particular thinking styles and to challenge them is important. If we consider George's thought processes in the context of the erroneous thinking styles listed above, we can see that George is catastrophising, disqualifying the positives and thinking in all or nothing terms. When mood is low, we also know that many individuals have a tendency to withdraw from others, to engage less meaningfully with life and to stop doing the very things that once provided us with pleasure. However, withdrawal tends to perpetuate the problem of mood. Instead, it is paramount that we do find meaningful and pleasurable new ways to create meaning and structure in our lives. This might involve seeking out a new activity that can provide some form of stimulation or interest, new friendships or companionship, developing hobbies or pleasurable pursuits, or transferring acquired skills to volunteering in some capacity. In essence, ensuring that life is sufficiently active and mentally stimulating will contribute to enduring psychological wellbeing in the longer term.

Loss, grief and bereavement

As you grow older, an inevitable aspect of life is facing your own mortality and that of those you love. Although this can happen at any time, when you become older the likelihood of experiencing a loss increases. When the loss of something or someone that you love or value occurs, you may experience intense emotional pain. This could apply to the loss of a relationship, your job or career, financial stability or entering into the process of retirement.

Often the most harrowing form of loss is that of someone we love. Grief is a very natural human response to bereavement and, although there is no typical response as we are all individuals and react as such, psychologists have proposed that there are certain common stages associated with the process of grief:

1. Denial: "This can't be happening ... it can't be true ..."
2. Anger: "Why? Who is to blame ... surely they could have done something ..."
3. Bargaining: "If he could come back I'd do anything ..."
4. Depression: "I feel too sad and empty ..."
5. Acceptance: "I feel at peace with what has happened ..."

These stages are not necessarily moved through in a linear fashion; they may be experienced in a somewhat more haphazard and chaotic way. For some individuals, a resolution of their grief may come about by experiencing none of the above stages. However, experiencing any or some of the above is certainly considered to be a normal reaction to the process of grief. It is thought that the stage of "acceptance" marks the coming to terms with the loss and all that it means.

Inevitably, bereavement can trigger a whole host of psychological symptoms that might prove a struggle to manage. The emotional weight of losing someone you love can also have a negative impact upon you physiologically, and it is inevitable you may struggle with some adverse symptoms, of both kinds.

Psychological symptoms:

- sadness – accompanied by strong feelings of emptiness, despair, loneliness, depression;
- shock – difficulty with processing and accepting what has happened;
- numbness – feeling shut off;
- guilt – experiencing regret about things you might have said or done differently;
- anger – feeling resentment towards self, others, higher powers (God) for what has happened;
- fear – feeling anxious and worried about the uncertainty of the future; and
- insecurity – feeling helpless and out of control of the present and future times.

Physiological symptoms:

- fatigue;
- nausea;

- headaches;
- loss of weight;
- minor ailments through lowered immunity;
- muscular pain;
- accelerated heartbeat;
- butterflies in the stomach; and
- restlessness.

Strategies for coping with loss

It is important to reassure yourself that the difficult symptoms that you are experiencing in relation to your loss are a normal part of the bereavement process. However, there is also the danger that a bereaved individual might position themselves entirely immersed in grief while becoming detached from the need to move forwards and engage with life again. This may lead to longer term depression. On the other hand, others may throw themselves into living and engaging with life in an otherwise unnatural way so as to avoid the process of grief. The healthiest form of grieving comes by finding a balance between the two extremes. There are a number of ways to do this: for example, working through the pain of grief, adjusting to the new environment, being able to form a helpful connection with the deceased through forming or developing friendships dear to the lost person, keeping cherished objects or memories, or having certain rituals and allocated times dedicated to that person's memory. These may all be helpful strategies, while you concurrently try to engage with life and find meaning, moving forwards to your best capacity.

Reaching out to others may also be helpful. Friends or family can be supportive or share your grief, which may be comforting. However, finding someone professional who can provide "talking therapy", such as a grief counsellor, may enable you to better understand your feelings and work through your grief. For some individuals, talking might not be of so much use, and distraction through keeping busy may be a more useful strategy. In any case, there are also a number of professional organisations designed to provide support to those struggling with grief, or indeed the practicalities of life after bereavement (see Resources).

Sleep problems

In general, it is normal for people to require less sleep as they get older. The quality of sleep is also affected and the tendency as you age is to have a more fragmented sleep and to be prone to being more easily roused. This is a natural process synonymous with growing older.

A number of factors may contribute to disturbed sleep patterns. A change of your routine, for example tending to go to bed later without the urgency to awake as early the next morning, can disrupt the circadian rhythm. A tendency to continue to wake early, however, might mean that you nap during the day to compensate for sleep lost overnight, which could develop as a habit, thereby perpetuating a sleep problem. Contending with significant life transitions can also contribute to changes in your sleeping patterns or habits. A change in your daily routine might result in you becoming less physically and mentally active during the day, so you feel less tired and ready to sleep at night.

Worrying about life changes, transitions, health issues, bereavement or indeed any other worries or concerns may also contribute to insomnia. As discussed earlier in this chapter, worrying thoughts contribute to feelings of anxiety, and these trigger the physiological symptoms that maintain the body's state of hyperarousal, which mean that the mind and body are unable to relax and fall asleep. The symptoms of insomnia can be:

- struggling to fall asleep;
- waking up during the night;
- waking up in the early hours of the morning and not being able to fall back to sleep; and
- feeling tired and restless, and experiencing impeded functioning during the day.

A number of sleep disorders may also get in the way of a restful night's sleep and contribute to longer term sleep disturbances. These include:

- sleep apnoea;
- restless leg syndrome; and
- periodic limb movement disorder.

Finally, lifestyle and unhelpful habits might contribute to disrupted sleep. The consumption of any form of stimulant may lead to a poor quality of sleep. These might include caffeine, nicotine or alcohol. Caffeine and nicotine might prevent one from falling asleep quickly, whereas alcohol might enable quick sleep but is disruptive for the second period of sleep as the body begins to metabolise the alcohol. Heavy meals and too much screen time too close to bedtime can also be disruptive to a good night's sleep.

Strategies for dealing with sleep problems

Sleep hygiene refers to good practices to maintain good quality night time sleep and alertness and ability to function adequately during the day. These practices include the following rules:

- Avoid stimulants such as caffeine, nicotine and alcohol to close to bedtime.
- Avoid napping during the day.
- Take plenty of exercise.
- Ensure sufficient exposure to natural daylight.
- Ensure bed is associated with sleep and sex (no other activity such as TV or radio).
- Avoid late meals close to bedtime.
- Avoid clock-watching.
- Remove anything that needs charging from the bedroom (mobile phone, e-book reader, laptop).
- Establish a relaxing bedtime routine (avoid stimulating conversation, problem solving or engaging in any emotion evoking activity).

If you can't fall asleep after 20 or 30 minutes, consider doing something practical for up to five minutes such as folding clothes, moving to your desk or lounge to read etc. Research has shown that the tendency to worry or ruminate tends to increase if you are unable to fall asleep within the first 20 minutes of going to bed. This can maintain sleep difficulties and it is therefore important to break the cycle by doing something different that will temporarily distract your mind.

Loneliness

Four out of ten pensioners, according to Age UK, feel lonely, and describe their television or their pet as their main company.

According to the Office of National Statistics, 43 per cent of people aged over 60 live on their own. Separation, divorce and bereavement can all lead to you living on your own, and families can move away or even abroad in search of work or affordable homes. Limited mobility, reduced income and perhaps not knowing your neighbours all contribute.

The charity Friends of the Elderly published a report looking at the landscape of loneliness for older people in the next five, ten and fifteen years. They found over 5 million older people in the UK are lonely, shockingly. Over the next fifteen years demographic change will see an increase in the number of lonely older people in the UK by another 40 per cent. One key factor appears to be contact with children; another is everyday contact with people.

Isolation is a particular issue for men, as the ILC found in its 2014 report, "Isolation: The emerging crisis for older men". The number of older men living alone is projected to rise by 65 per cent, to 1.5 million, between now and 2030. Older men tend to be more socially isolated than older women, and have significantly less contact with their family and friends. They define "loneliness" as a subjective perception in which a person feels lonely, whereas "social isolation" refers to the absence of contact with other people.

Recent research presented at the American Association for the Advancement of Science has shown that loneliness affects our physical health, not just our mental well-being. It can be twice as unhealthy as obesity, according to research by John Cacioppo, an American psychologist who warns against people approaching retirement age moving home. Similarly, it can be as damaging as smoking 15 cigarettes a day, according to Marianne Symons of the Campaign to End Loneliness, which is publicising these health risks and lobbying for research funding.

Social isolation can lead to heart disease, arthritis, type II diabetes and an impaired immune system, as well as depression, stress, dementia and lethargy. Quite how worrying this is can be underlined by the fact that those charities and organisations combatting social isolation are now getting more attention and financial resources from the government, in an attempt to deflect the potential financial burden on the state.

A few people are content with isolation, and some people feel lonely even when surrounded by family and friends. So, living alone doesn't necessarily equate to loneliness, but a third of people over 50 and nearly half over 80 are always or often lonely. These statistics indicate an epidemic of loneliness, and it will only get worse.

According to Emily White, loneliness blogger and author, "Loneliness is a serious and intense state; you have to recognise that getting over it will take both work and time."

Strategies to help you deal with loneliness

Loneliness is a huge issue, affecting large numbers of people of all ages but particularly the elderly, and it can affect our health. But it doesn't have to be like that. We've got lots of suggestions for you so you need never be lonely.

It is important to plan against loneliness, with elements in your life set up and pre-arranged to ensure sociability and contact with others on a variety of levels. Here are some ideas for things you can do to help yourself.

Social media

Social media can be a wonderful tool for keeping in touch with people. Caroline Abrahamson of Age UK says, "a lot of older people live alone, so reaching out online, particularly if you're not as mobile as you used to be, is a good way of keeping in touch with friends and family".

The ILC's Europe's Ageing Demography report shows that over 80 per cent of 55- to 64-year-olds and about 65 per cent of 65- to 74-year-olds accessed the Internet in the UK in 2013, considerably higher than in many other European countries.

Many older people find Skype in particular is a boon for maintaining contact with family abroad. However, social media can also be isolating if you start to feel your life is lacking compared to others; it is important to remember that not everything posted on Facebook is true!

Friends of the Elderly found that technology does have the potential to have a positive impact on loneliness. However, according to their survey, by the year 2030 one in 10 of older people will still not have a mobile phone or use the Internet.

Neighbours

Friends of the Elderly's "Be a Friend" campaign encourages connection with neighbours and communities and suggests people start by having a chat with an older neighbour over the garden fence, offering to help with shopping and everyday tasks, and sharing knowledge and ideas. When that older person is you, obviously how you respond to these initial modes of contact can make a large difference in the longer term. Other charities run services to beat loneliness, such as Coffee Companions.

Other small steps you can take include inviting several neighbours for tea to discuss a charitable project, or hosting a home shopping event. In addition, reach out to others who may be in the same position as yourself and suggest joint trips to the shops, theatre or cinema.

Clubs

- Age UK (www.ageuk.org.uk). Caroline Abrahamson of Age UK says "if you can easily get out and about, think about joining a local organisation aimed at people your age. Age UK runs a variety of fitness classes and groups."
- Contact the Elderly (www.contact-the-elderly.org.uk) run monthly tea parties for the over-75s as does NBFA Assisting the Elderly.

- The University of the Third Age (U3A, www.u3a.org.uk) has local groups based on learning, where members share skills and teach each other, plus social activities
- The Royal Voluntary Service (www.royalvoluntaryservice.org.uk) has social clubs for the elderly nationwide.
- In addition, investigate alumni – your university, company or industry may well have one, plus industry-specific clubs and societies that would welcome your experience and involvement.

Lonely hearts

- *Saga Magazine* has a column for advertisements by single people.
- Try dating websites such as www.justseniorsingles.com or matureda tinguk.com

Befriending services

- Age UK (www.ageuk.org.uk).
- Friends of the Elderly (www.fote.org.uk).
- Independent Age (www.independentage.org).
- The Silver Line (www.thesilverline.org.uk).

Anti-loneliness projects

A number of projects have been set up to help tackle loneliness:

- One project – Tyneside-based HenPower – has been awarded a £1 million National Lottery grant to roll out its initiative across Britain. HenPower gives elderly people, known as "hensioners", chickens to look after, which gives them a sense of purpose, and improves their health and wellbeing. The delicious eggs help too!
- The Big Lottery Fund has awarded grants to several innovative projects. One project led by animators Creature Comforts and Age UK Bristol is spending £6 million to tackle social isolation among 12,000 older people in Bristol including creating an animation to help change public perception of this issue.
- Another charity, the Silver Line (see above), founded by Esther Rantzen with the aim of combatting loneliness in old age, received more than 100,000 calls in its first 12 months to its free 24-hour telephone befriending and advice service following a £5 million grant.
- The National Endowment for Science, Technology and the Arts has an Ageing Well Challenge Prize. The five 2013 finalists included projects for a radio club, a comfort food and community café, a postretirement club for men, a support group for older LGBT people in London and a project in Exeter to help men with complex

needs repair sheds and tools to send to UK charities and African business start-ups. They declare that growing old is mandatory – but isolation doesn't have to be.

> Ask yourself: What can I start doing now to mitigate the prospect of loneliness in the future?

By the way, to reduce the risk of becoming lonely in the future, try to have more than one interest in your life. This means you have a backup plan, and are not wholly dependent on one thing. For example, if you enjoy pottery at the local college but the funding stops and there is nowhere else within reach, you will be left high and dry.

Addictions

The use of drugs and alcohol is not uncommon among older adults during the retirement period. For some this might be a continuation of previous lifestyle and use of substances; for others, it may represent a newly developing relationship. As noted previously, navigating a new chapter of your lifespan with the host of challenges that can be attached to this may contribute to some difficult emotional experiences such as loneliness, grief, anxiety and low mood. The use of alcohol and drugs can provide an escape from troublesome feelings, but inevitably also creates its own problems.

It is not always feelings of misery and despair that drives people towards substance dependence. Having an attitude towards retirement as being the time to relax, enjoy and having earned the right to indulge in pleasures might also lead to complacency around the use of alcohol. It is a central nervous system depressant and has a major effect on weight and general health. There is perhaps a greater sense of social acceptance around being able to have a good drink at the golf club, for example, a type of hard-earned reward or sense of deserving to have a "good time" after years of hard work and raising a family. For those enjoying alcohol as part of a social life or "vacation" type of lifestyle post retirement, it is important to not become complacent as a habit can inadvertently develop into a dependency with physical and psychological consequences. Excessive use of alcohol can have detrimental physical and psychological outcomes.

Consider the following case example.

> Thomas, a retired chief executive officer, feels a loss of identity with retirement and withdraws socially, drinks more than usual

and becomes physically inactive. This leads to increased levels of unhappiness. We challenged this downward spiral and the stereotypes of the retired person he was holding on to.

Table 4.1 illustrates how negative thoughts can affect different aspects of our behaviour and thoughts, but are also susceptible to challenge. After all, they are ideas or beliefs or feelings and actions/behaviour and if we address them differently this may produce different outcomes. The table illustrates this by first highlighting some stereotypes and how these present, and then posing and suggesting some alternative ones that Thomas can consider so that thoughts do not become self-fulfilling.

It is also worth noting that, in older adults, drug dependency is much more likely to refer to prescription medication than illicit drugs. As medication is prescribed for physical or psychological illness, it can be easy for the use of such medication to gradually transform into a relationship of dependence, especially insofar as sedatives or opiates are concerned.

Table 4.1 Thomas's reflections about his own situation

	Presentation	*Psychological intervention*
Thoughts	Because I am no longer the CEO no one will be interested in me or include me	Challenge beliefs and assumptions about retirement, old age and identity that developed from family stories
Feelings	Low mood, anxiety, dread, hopelessness, anger, frustration, boredom	More hopeful that experience could change; more connected to others
Behaviour	Lack of activity, socially withdrawn, excess use of alcohol	Develop a range of activities which bring pleasure and a sense of achievement. Become more socially engaged and engaging in marriage
Physiology	Lethargic, hung-over, depleted immune system, decrease in physical fitness	More energy, fitness
Outcome	Excess alcohol use; this puts strain on relationships. Increased sense of isolation. Lack of activity fuels beliefs about retirement being bleak and negative beliefs about oneself	Improved relationships, increased self-esteem and self-efficacy, mood increased and anxiety reduced

The use of alcohol, prescription medication or illicit drugs to combat difficult feelings may numb out the emotions in the shorter term, but may lead to a long-term addiction and both psychological and physiological difficulties.

> Ask yourself: Am I likely to start drinking too much when I retire?

Addictive behaviour has many forms. Some people shop addictively, with rooms full of unworn clothing. Gambling can also become a problem (including dishonesty, and causing financial hardship and poverty) and many people use it as a way to channel their agitation. It is also common for people of all ages to become addicted to social media or the Internet (including surfing for porn). One of the main issues with overuse of the Internet and social media is that your life will be too sedentary. Moving more will help you become more positive. We have some tips for exercising in Chapter 8.

Excessive travel is a form of addictive behaviour more common in those of retirement age than other age groups. Many people celebrate retirement with a cruise or a grand trip, either to explore or to see far-flung friends and relatives. Some though take this too far and are constantly planning, packing, unpacking or actually away. This can have a detrimental effect on your relationships at home. We all know how boring it can be looking at endless holiday snaps or videos, but if you don't have anything else to talk about and become disconnected with those back home, possibly even alienating them by appearing to be showing off, you could end up isolated.

Other potential downsides of excessive travel include:

- Financial implications, if you haven't saved up enough money for the trip.
- The risk that the only way we can feel fulfilled is to constantly have adventures. Perhaps we're avoiding something at home – stability, predictability, fear of being still or alone, or with our partner.
- If you want to explore the world a great tip is to plan to travel more earlier on in your retirement when it will be easier to get travel insurance. The cost of this goes up hugely with age and medical conditions, making it prohibitively expensive or even impossible in some cases. In addition, flying is also an unknown quantity in terms of what it does to your health if you already have health issues.

- Too much transmeridian travel (long-haul, crossing time zones) can be disruptive to our thought patterns and mental sharpness.

Strategies for coping with addictions

Logic dictates that, if something is addictive and harmful, then we should stop doing it. If only this were as simple in some cases. The strongest drivers or factors that maintain additive behaviours are as follows:

1 Having nothing meaningful to replace or displace the addictive behaviour.
2 Poor levels of motivation to change.
3 Related factors not being adequately addressed (e.g. boredom, leading to a sedentary lifestyle, leading to disappearing into one's room to switch on your computer, leading to surfing for porn, leading to extended time spent doing this, and then online porn becomes the main or only sexual outlet).
4 Genetic and inherited factors.
5 Getting away with the addictive behaviours, by others turning a blind eye, their not being aware of the extent or even presence of the addiction which could introduce deceit into a relationship, and not confronting the person about their addiction for fear of making it worse or driving it underground.

Some specialists who treat addictions do not recommend "coping" with addictions and assert that nothing short of complete abstinence should be the goal for anyone seeking help. This may be a requirement for the successful treatment of certain addictions and addictive behaviours as the risk of slipping back into old ways if we only reduce them is ever present. The starting point for self-treatment is simply and honestly to recognise that you are addicted to something. This doesn't require much more than an honest recognition that the behaviour controls you more than you control it. And, furthermore, that it is disrupting other parts of your life (your wallet, your relationships, your sex life, your health etc.) and is taking up too much time. For some people, this may be enough to curb things.

The next step is to find the motivation to change the behaviour. Identify and keep a clear goal in mind. Perhaps it could be to give up alcohol for three months to see what this does to you. Incentives should be clear and measurable, and gains should be able to be made rapidly. Some behaviour change programmes fail because the goals and targets take far too long to come about. Someone seeking to lose 30 kilos in weight is hardly likely to achieve this in the course of a normal three-month diet. It would be better to aim for, say, a kilo in weight loss per fortnight at the very most.

Lifestyle changes also need to be made. Find new activities to replace the addictive behaviours. The list of possibilities is endless, of course, but ensure there are some things you can do almost immediately, at odd hours when addictive urges might be at their strongest, and which are satisfying. Where you can, engage others in these activities too, so you have a reason to do them; this will also help to anchor your activities in social interaction. And remember to stay away from objects that are linked to your addiction – your computer if it's online addictions, or, as some do, cut up your bank card or freeze it in a block of ice, if that's the method you use to draw cash for the casino.

If you feel daring, tell others what you are planning to do. By sharing your goals, you can enlist the support of friends and family in bringing about changes in your life. They can motivate you, distract you, chastise you if you need a reminder to keep on track, and also help break the sense of isolation and shame that sometimes accompanies these addictions and also the process of change itself. Remember to reward yourself for the changes you succeed in bringing about. The value of a reward is of course quite personal, but those with whom we have worked professionally have taken luxury holidays, bought a new set of golf clubs, taken up flying lessons, undergone elective plastic surgery, got a dog, enjoyed the benevolence of helping others with their addictions; the list is endless.

As is highlighted elsewhere in this book, there are some problems that require more specialist help if we are to change or overcome them. There are addictions specialists, and a visit to your GP or going online to look for a therapist is a start. Imagine yourself actually eyeballing a professional and saying to them "I have a problem with alcohol", or "I think I'm addicted to gambling". Now you've taken that step by hearing yourself saying you have a problem, you have more than one foot in the door of change. How scary. How exciting! Good luck.

Retirement in our contemporary age can prove to be an exciting time that, if well prepared for, can provide the opportunity to pursue new interests and projects. However, like any part of life it can present us with particular challenges that if not managed effectively may, in the worst-case scenarios, lead to psychological distress. As discussed throughout this chapter, understanding and addressing erroneous and unhelpful thinking and self-defeating behaviour is important for minimising any negative psychological impact. Ensuring daily structure and engagement in activities and behaviour that ultimately provide stimulation and pleasure will help to contribute towards a more meaningful existence throughout your retirement years.

But despite all your best efforts, you might still be sabotaged by your emotions. In Chapter 5, we take a brief look at the range of emotions that might arise in retirement, and give you tools to help deal with these.

Chapter 5

Retirement and emotions

Retirement can be a time of mixed emotions. For some it is a dream; for others, something to dread, or it can be a combination of these feelings. And it is complicated, as feelings can be welcome or unwelcome, or sometimes both. Here are some examples of these feelings:

- Welcome feelings – satisfaction at having raised a family, paid the mortgage, looking forward to new work, hobbies, activities and adventures.
- Less welcome feelings – a time beset with fear and anxiety; a sense of futility and depression; boredom and existential questions.

Therefore, this is a life stage where coping and resilience may be demanded.

As human beings we experience a myriad of emotions. Here are just a few you might find you are feeling more than usual as retirement approaches.

Loss

As you get older there is more to lose. Loss can encompass loss of your job/identity; loss of your future through illness; loss due to the death of a loved one; a sense of loss when children leave home; loss of mobility; loss of autonomy and space. We discussed psychological approaches to loss in the previous chapter.

Emotional stress

You might find you experience emotional stress due to a "reconfiguration" of your relationship with your partner and/or children. For more on relationships see the next chapter.

Low mood

Retirement can also be a time when we suffer from low moods. In particular, there is a link between low levels of exercise and low moods. We discussed psychological approaches to low mood in the previous chapter. Here are some more suggested strategies:

- Smile! You can't feel down if you are smiling. And if you find smiling hard, look up – raising your eyes automatically generates an uplifting smile.
- Change what you do habitually. For example, sit on a different chair, change the order you do things, or the day on which you do them. Take a different route somewhere; try a new breakfast cereal; wear a new colour; move off with your left foot. Breaking a routine breaks mental habits. If you do things differently you will feel differently, so take action and you will be happy then.

Waiting for your feelings to improve is an inefficient way of making yourself feel better. And waiting for someone else to do it for you won't get you anywhere. Make sure you have something to get out of bed for, and take physical exercise to give you a boost. And as soon as you get a lift that suggests things are moving the right way, you will become yet more positive.

Uncertainty

We discussed uncertainty in the previous chapter in relation to anxiety, worry and fear, especially of change.

Unhappiness

Happiness is what we are all aiming for, isn't it? So many of us are dissatisfied, as we perceive we are not "happy". But do you really know what happiness means for you?

> Ask yourself: What would make you happy?

A study by Lara Aknin and colleagues in the *Journal of Positive Psychology* found that many people believe that money can buy you extra happiness. Economist Justin Wolfers shows a strong correlation between income and happiness, but psychologist Daniel Kahneman and economist Angus Deaton found that happiness does not continue to increase above incomes of $75,000 a year. Money does bring more choices; however, too much choice can actually be more frustrating than exciting, according to a Newsweek article.

Friends and family are worth more than status purchases. The prices of non-marketable goods, such as friendship or marriage provide greater happiness than marketable goods. The 75-year longitudinal Harvard Grant Study into what makes us happy came up with the answer that ... what makes us happy is doing things that make us happy, such as spending time with loved ones and friends.

Money and status do not make people happy. Winning the lottery won't make you instantly happy: it takes years to enjoy the benefits, and it means that you are out of sync with friends and family. We do, however, feel differently about hard-earned pension money, as we see it as a reward, and we tend to have been looking forward to it for a long time!

The secret to being happy is simply to devote more of our time and attention to happiness in the form of rich and fulfilling experiences. This usually lies in what we already have and enjoy – time with friends and family. Revisit your life goals, and plan ways to work towards achieving these.

Many people believe their happiness depends on external factors, but changes in our behaviour can make us happier. These are things we can do to help ourselves. Try to minimise or avoid behavioural extremes and addictive behaviour. You may also want to consider writing down your feelings as this can help you to process the issues that are causing negative emotions. Keeping a regular diary allows you to "share" your feelings which can be especially productive if you find it difficult to open up to friends and family. Each entry does not have to be long. Instead focus on documenting how you are feeling and what you are thinking on that particular day.

Many of the emotional issues we have discussed here can be allayed by having a good set of relationships, at home, in the community and so on. We discuss relationships, and the impact retirement has on them, in the next chapter.

Chapter 6

The impact on relationships

Retirement not only affects your internal state of mind; it also affects your external relationships. And it impacts on others in ways that are not always obvious. In addition, many of the challenges of retirement are personal and impact on your family.

The impact

Retirement impacts on relationships in a variety of ways:

- Retirement often places significant stress on relationships.
- Relationships are normally a buffer against stress.
- There is heightened need (and time) for social interaction; this may place stress on relationships.
- Emotional, social and financial needs and expectations may differ.
- Goals for retirement may not be shared.
- Communication may go awry.
- Physical/sexual intimacy needs may change or not be calibrated.
- Challenges to emotional stability may spill over into relationships.

Skipton Building Society commissioned research in 2015 (https://www.skipton.co.uk/~/media/skipton-co-uk/pdf/Retirement/RetirementIndex Interactive2015.ashx?la=en-GB) into relationships in retirement. The statistics are revealing. Eighty per cent of respondents in a relationship admitted their relationship had lost its spark, and they were no longer sharing hobbies and interests with their partner. One third of couples argued a lot about small things, with 13 per cent irritating each other "beyond belief". Forty per cent had to find a new way of living together post work. Couples can find it hard to adjust to spending every hour together. A quarter of retirees found their relationship harder to manage than they had thought. Half of the respondents were worried about money and a fifth argued about different attitudes towards money, with one spending and the other saving.

Arguments were common. Eleven per cent argued about how to spend their time; other arguments started from interfering with cooking, disagreeing about time spent on the telephone, and contrasting energy levels. Surprisingly, perhaps, 90 per cent of couples saw these differences as merely a "temporary glitch", and thought they would eventually settle into happy retirement together.

Stacey Stothard of the Skipton Building Society concluded:

> Without a doubt, a key part of a happy retirement is planning. Couples who plan their retirement ambitions together are likely to argue less and enjoy each other's company more when they stop work. But planning shouldn't start the moment you retire – in fact, the earlier you think about it the better.

> Ask yourself: What thoughts/concerns do you have about spending more time at home? Are there particular situations or dynamics you find difficult to deal with? If so, what are these? What are the positive aspects of your relationships with your partner, children, friends or grandchildren?

As highlighted in our first chapter, retirement is both an individual process that affects your inner sense of wellbeing and achievement among many other processes. It also has a profound impact on relationships and not least your relationship with your partner, loved ones and those at home. It is potentially a high-risk error to ignore the consequences of retirement on those around you. Planning for retirement should always give consideration to the likely impact on others of your stopping work and potentially being at home more, if some obvious and less expected problems are to be avoided.

Consider the following case example.

> Phillip, a hotelier, and his wife Naomi, who have been married for 40 years, regard themselves as a typical and traditional couple. They met at school, married within a few years and had their first children in their early twenties. They have always enjoyed family life and Phillip has always been ambitious, although not necessarily to be at the very top of the organisation in which he has been employed. He has worked for a hotel group for the greater part of his adult life. Over this time, Naomi raised their three children and looked after their domestic matters. Naomi was responsible for the children's schooling, and

fetching and carrying them from their friends and extracurricular activities. She was house-proud, ensuring that their home was always tidy and the fridge well stocked. She developed some of her own interests, including glass blowing, teaching English as a foreign language to students, enrolling on a number of different cooking courses and also more recently completing part-time counselling training. While not obliged to retire at the age of 65, Phillip had always planned for this from a financial perspective; and, in terms of what the couple wanted to enjoy in later life, it made sense to keep to this milestone.

Three months before retirement, it dawned on Naomi that her initial excitement about Phillip's impending retirement was becoming tainted by an increasing anxiety about the prospect of him being at home. As much as he had made excellent financial and practical provisions for his retirement, he had not developed his social network sufficiently and his hobby interests had never properly got off the ground and reflected more tinkering with different possibilities. Naomi was worried that his presence at home would unsettle their relationship. She was concerned that he would literally get under her feet and his lack of external interests would make him more dependent on her for his social life and entertainment. She felt conflicted about this feeling as she did not want to unsettle or hurt him by expressing her anxieties about this impending sense of claustrophobia, but on the other hand felt it was important that he started to develop external interests.

As a first measure the couple sat and discussed their dilemma. Their grown-up children had left home, so they decided that they would both have their own separate study at home with their own computers so they could manage their own business, correspondence and financial affairs. It also afforded them a symbolic separation of their matters and divided their personal space. Phillip spoke to some friends who had recently retired and listened carefully to their advice about pre-retirement planning. He realised that with only three months to go it would be difficult to take up completely new interests and begin to engage in these fully and master them. However, he also recognised that in order to develop and sustain the relationships he had already formed in the town, it would be wise to take up one or two interests that resembled those of the others that he had met with. He started his first round of golf lessons within a week and also transferred his gym membership closer to home, but not so close that he could just walk there – it would entail a small journey in order to get there.

The couple also bought a diary (they were not keen on using an online version, which would have been ideal), in which appointments and activities would be pencilled in. They would therefore both have a visual reminder of the planned week's activities ahead of time and they encouraged one another to do as much away from home as possible. They also made it a ritual to have lunch together once a week outside of the home. They started to approach the whole retirement phase issue about how time and space would be managed by thinking "When would we like to be together this week and what would we like to do then?" as opposed to "What can I do with my spare time?"

In the first instance, you need to have a conversation about the shape of life in the retirement phase. Do not simply cross your fingers and hope it will be a seamless process as you withdraw from work and assume you will be happily and comfortably embraced at home. Assuming that "it will be business as usual and normal" at home does not take into account the feelings of others.

Retirement highlights many important, sensitive and complex relationship dynamics. For each individual there is an issue about separateness and togetherness. Being at work engenders some level of separateness but the assumption that togetherness, on retirement, is welcomed by both partners or other family members is not always the case. Many couples we have spoken to expressed mixed feelings about retirement. There may be some fear or dread about being together and spending more time with one another when the relationship has worked well thus far with a level of separateness to sustain it. Being together places undue pressure that may not have existed at any time previously in the relationship, or certainly not for many years prior to retirement. One or both partners leaving home to go to work (or having separate rooms to work from at home) may have afforded the necessary separateness needed in order to enjoy a balanced life. Many people feel the need to work, not only for financial benefit and mental stimulation, but also as way to maintain a healthy relationship with their partner through the natural ebb and flow of the comings and goings that work and home schedules bring.

There may be some level of concern or worry that the relationship may run out of steam or feel claustrophobic or overwhelming as a result of spending time together. There could be small niggling points of overlap where we literally physically or emotionally bump into one another. Things used to work according to a certain routine and plan before retirement but the presence of another person at home may lead to conflict or expectations about roles and how things will be carried out there. In addition, there may be different goals about the period of retirement. For example, one person may look forward to retirement as a period in which more time can be spent with children or grandchildren, whereas the other partner may be looking forward to travel, hobbies outside of family life and spending as much of the day away from home as possible. Without discussion or negotiation, our respective goals and dreams may be thwarted, giving rise to unpleasant and potentially relationship challenging feelings.

Many couples we have spoken to express fear of the unknown. They worry about sharing physical space, about being controlled by their partner and by potential for loss of identity. They express concerns that they will need to put effort into a relationship, whereas before work helped to moderate it. There are concerns sometimes that there will be boredom and that this could have a detrimental and draining effect on the relationship. Encroachment on your partner's time, space and routines could be unwelcome and lead to unhappiness and disrupted patterns of attachment. There may be pressure to carry out mundane tasks at home, which may not be fulfilling and are therefore avoided.

At a practical level, roles may need to be shared. As one couple expressed to us, there would be extra cleaning to do having someone else around at home. Pets may become an issue: one partner may want to get a pet that they have not been able to look after during their working life, or there may be an expectation about who walks the dog and whether this is done as a couple together or separately. Some couples have little choice in their retirement activities. They may be required to look after elderly parents or sickly children. The expectation of having more time may not immediately be realised.

Many people are socially inclined and during their working life enjoyed the company and engagement of people around them. Spending more time at home or in one's community can at times feel claustrophobic and overwhelming. Compromise may need to be sought in order to ensure that everyone's needs are best met and not just those of the retiree.

The process of how things get done at home may also differ. If one of the partners has largely looked after home life, there may be a measure of resentment about the retiree taking over responsibility for getting things done. The method and timescale in which they do things may differ from how they were done previously bringing the couple more into conflict.

It almost goes without question that relationships will come under close scrutiny and face a number of new pressures and challenges. If these are not addressed and discussed at an early stage – or better still before retirement, there is a risk that the very relationship that we have dreamt about spending more time in and which theoretically and practically should provide a buffer against life stresses, will itself become a source of stress (see also *Feeling Good Together* by David D. Burns). Let's consider another case example.

David, a university researcher, and Bill, a publisher, were married in New York in 2014. They had lived together in a relationship for 22 years. As a couple, they enjoyed doing many things together and, every time they had conversations in which they discussed and planned for their future, retirement was always conceived as something they would do together. Before giving up their jobs, they thought it wise to seek couples counselling to ensure that they were making the best decision for themselves. The following was recorded from the session.

David: "I need to be absorbed in activities, I can't see myself just doing nothing in retirement."

Bill: "Yes, I fear passivity. I think doing things such as reading books or going to movies is too passive. I need to do something. I need to get out into the garden. I need to set things up. I need to keep busy. I need a retirement that involves doing things."

David: "Yes I agree, leisure things are much more fun when you can use them to switch off from something else. I know I will go to the gym often but going to the gym now is a great way to relax and chill out. I don't think it will feel quite the same when I retire."

Bill: "Absolutely, variety is really important for me too."

David: "Yes, it's a bit like drinking champagne. It is only really good because you don't drink it all the time. If it becomes what you do every day then it loses its sense of specialness."

Bill: "Being around younger people is important to me. In my job there has been a lot of that and it's always kept me on my toes and made me feel more interested in what I do. There is also the tyranny of the timesheet. I hate filling out timesheets and being in servitude to someone else. I also certainly won't miss the lowness of Sunday evenings when I sometimes have to think about the working week ahead and also the regulatory environment in which I have been."

David: "Yeah, I can think of quite a few things that I won't miss in my job but I also think about what I would say to others. What if somebody asks, 'what is your job?' I can't say nothing. My job is also my identity and I don't want people to think of me as having a big void in my life."

Bill: "Yeah, keeping busy mentally is perhaps the most important thing, but maybe we don't have to do everything together. Perhaps it's a misguided aim that we think that retirement means that we will spend all of our time doing the same activities and sharing the same time and space with the same friends and so on. Maybe what we need to think about is to turn it on its head and that is to continue to do things separately but to plan for those times when we are together. That can help up to focus on how to respect one another's space."

> Ask yourself: What impact is your retirement likely to have on those around you?

Relationship tips

1 Make retirement a relationship issue, not just a personal one.
2 Plan ahead; ensure everyone's needs are addressed.
3 Identify points of conflict and work to resolve them.
4 Identify areas of shared interest and commonality (e.g. finances, grandparent role, etc.).
5 Resolve differences over time spent with friends and neighbours.
6 Focus on the problem, not the person. Don't personalise or make accusations.
7 Address (don't ignore) sexual problems.
8 Manage your mood/mind proactively so boredom, stress or low mood does not spill over.
9 Proactively manage health issues and concerns.
10 Address complex and sensitive issues such as fear of loss.
11 Consider couple or family therapy if you and your partner/family are struggling to overcome relationship difficulties.

Develop separateness

Retirement is not necessarily about togetherness. Doing things separately is key to a lasting and satisfying relationship.

Establish new rituals to preserve separateness: hobbies, friends, activities. This means you will always have something new to say to each other. It also reduces dependency and strengthens not only your relationship but also prepares you for the time when one of you will be left alone.

Gender, sex and problems

It is best to avoid stereotypes here as, metaphorically speaking, "one size doesn't fit all". There is no "ideal" or "perfect" relationship; and there is no "ideal" or "perfect" sexual relationship. Not all couples have sex. Not all couples have regular sex. Not all couples enjoy sex the same each time. Not all sex is intense and fulfilling. Not all relationships are monogamous. Not all sexual behaviours with the same person are fulfilling. By now you have probably got the gist; this is too complex and sensitive an area to be prescriptive or to reflect "the norm". In fact, these phrases are likely to be the source of the problem or difficulty if this section relates to you. It's a stereotype (but possibly accurate to some situations) that men find the physical aspects of sex more compelling than the emotional aspects and that women want sex to be sensual and prolonged. It's also a stereotype (but, again, possibly true for some) that gay men want lots of sex and that some prefer anonymous sexual encounters. Sex is too complex a topic to frame neatly or for that matter to gloss over lightly.

Everyone is likely at some point in their lives – whether in or out of a relationship – to question their sexual behaviours (or lack of sex), sexual feelings, what intimacy might feel like with a different partner, possibly their sexuality, and even whether they still feel sexually inclined or aroused. Some of the biggest problems we see with people who seek professional help for relationship and sexual problems is a worry that they are not meeting the needs of their partner, that their partner may no longer arouse them, or that everyone else seems to be having a better time with their intimacy and that they must be doing something wrong. To disavow someone of such fears is often half the difficulty overcome. Expectations, comparisons, the perception of "normal" and fears of not doing things right are at the heart of many sexual problems.

As we get older, some sexual behaviours may change. We may want sex less often. Physical ailments can get in the way. Some couples don't share a bed due to a health or snoring difficulty. Libido or sex drive may change. Mood and alcohol problems may disrupt the enjoyment of sexual intimacy. We may struggle to admit that, after many years, our partner does not meet all of our sexual needs. Or, having sex outside of our primary relationship might be more erotic or fulfilling. There is no right or wrong here; there are feelings and each may have some validity.

When we are in an enduring relationship (marriage, civil partnership, cohabitation), it is often difficult to disentangle sex and desire from what is happening in our relationship. Accordingly, sexual problems, for many people in a relationship, are by definition also relationship problems. By addressing one, you are probably simultaneously dealing with the other. It is important therefore to treat sex difficulties with sensitivity and to recognise that they will likely inevitably reach into your relationship.

The starting point, as is the case with many personal problems, is to recognise and define the problem. In some instances, it is a clear and specific symptom, such as pain during intercourse, premature ejaculation, lack of sex drive, delayed ejaculation, or the unexpected presence of blood which is spooky and worrying. Every doctor is trained in communications skills and in taking a sexual history, so a visit to your GP or a sexual health clinic might be a start, but probably preceded by a chat with your partner if embarrassment and shame are not overriding features. The treatment of sexual problems either through medications, cognitive behavioural therapy, couples therapy, sensate focus (a specific technique for enhancing sex and intercourse) or in some cases minor surgery is much advanced. There should be no need for the vast majority of men, women, heterosexual or same sex couples to endure sexual problems, and treatment can often be swift and effective.

Problems that stem from attraction, ageing, underlying relationship difficulties and secondary health problems may appear to be less specific than some of those listed above, but they are no less treatable in many cases. The book *Feeling Good Together* by David Burns is an excellent starting point in self-help. You may need to identify your goal or outcome for the difficulty in order to treat it appropriately. Do you want more sex? Longer-lasting sex? Sex that is enhanced by medications to help with erectile difficulties or erotic feelings (women now have Addyi, the "pink pill", to match men's Viagra and related erectile treatments)? Introducing sex aids to intimate acts? Having sex in a different place and not in the bedroom? More frequent sex? Sex with someone other than your partner? Apologies if this sounds like a shopping list from which you should choose! It is simply intended to highlight that you need to identify what you want to be different if there is such a need. And you probably need to discuss this with your partner if you want this to be done consensually and with the best chance of success, to avoid introducing new difficulties into your relationship.

It is a complete myth that, as we get older, sex wanes for everyone. Intimacy needs may change. Our bodies may function a bit differently. We may look at our partner differently. But it may also be a time of less fraught sex and more mutually enjoyable and satisfying sex. So, whether you are in or out of a relationship, gay or straight, bisexual, transgendered, 87 years of age, man or woman, still working or properly retired, if sex is an issue, do something to change it! Good sex is good for your psychological health, physical health, relationship(s) and sense of wellbeing. Sex is good, if you like it; and it's good for you too.

Preventing relationship breakdown and divorce

There is an increase in marriages of people aged over 65, named "silver splicers" by *The Times* (https://www.thetimes.co.uk/article/silver-splicers-make-sixty-the-new-sexy-lh87snwhtxp), up by 46 per cent in the decade to 2014, according to the most recent ONS marriage data [taken from https://www.ons.gov.uk/peoplepopulationandcommunity/birthsdeathsandmarriages/marriagecohabitationandcivilpartnerships/articles/marriageanddivorceontheriseat65andover/2017-07-18]. Virtually all (92 per cent) of those aged 65 or more in 2014 were divorcees, widows or widowers, with a mere 8 per cent getting married for the first time.

However, these is also an increase in what the *Guardian* terms "silver separators" (https://www.theguardian.com/lifeandstyle/shortcuts/2015/nov/24/silver-separators-over-50s-divorce-splitting-up-children). It is a sad fact that many couples divorce, and the divorce rate for married men and women over the age of 55 is continuing to increase, despite average divorce rates in every other age group starting to fall (by 2.9 per cent in 2012 -13). All these figures can be at least partly accounted for by people living longer and the closing of the gender gap in life expectancy; later divorces are also influenced by the timing of children leaving home.

The legal process of getting divorced is considerably easier than it used to be, although it can still inflict great financial pain as well as emotional hurt. For those married more than 20 years the starting point is 50 per cent of the net matrimonial worth.

Being divorced is far more socially acceptable, with barely any stigma nowadays at all, especially for the post-war generation. Now we are all living longer and 60 is no longer considered old, staying in an unhappy or unfulfilling marriage for another 20 or 30 years after retirement is far from the only option, particularly for women. Empty nest syndrome is a big trigger for women, far more so than the finding of a new partner. Men tend to instigate divorce so they can be with somebody else

Counselling can sometimes prevent divorce, but preparation for retirement has a far greater role. A counsellor can advise couples to discuss their visions of the future, both as individuals and as a couple. Relationship counsellor and author Barbara Bloomfield offers the following advice:

> There are an awful lot of women out there fed up with a grumpy man, and vice versa. Perhaps they have been putting up with strife and bickering for a long, long time. But although it's harder to change patterns of behaviour as we get older, it is not impossible to learn new tricks and find a new energy and spark.

> Ask yourself: Is your marriage/relationship likely to survive the changes and challenges of retirement? What do you think are the factors that may help you and your family deal with the changes of retirement? Are there any additional things/support you and your family can do to ease the process of retirement?

One useful tool offered by Relate is an online Relationship MOT Quiz (https://www.relate.org.uk/relationship-help/help-relationships/feeling-unsatisfied-your-relationship/relationship-mot-quiz). This very short questionnaire is designed to reveal how healthy your marriage really is. Relate's partner organisation, Marriage Care, has launched a 50+ couples intervention programme to help with the transition to retirement (https://www.marriagecare.org.uk/how-we-help/couple-50-mot/).

Chapter 7

Moving on from work

Leaving the workplace

Leaving work is often difficult. As we mentioned in Chapter 1, you may lose your sense of identity and status. Without work as an anchor, you may feel vulnerable. Leaving work might make you feel old and useless, and you might start to worry about ageing. Your feelings may be affected by whether you are being "pushed out", causing resentment, or whether it is a planned and amicable departure.

You may feel satisfaction at what you have achieved in your life, or be looking forward to spending time doing things you have always wanted to do, such as hobbies or seeing friends. However, it is a natural human tendency around this time to be pessimistic and you might tend to dwell on the past and regrets. In addition, you may become fearful of the future. But you need to develop resilience to this. You may also feel a sense of loss.

Changes and losses of status and identity are important because work provides you with a sense of fulfilment, control and structure – it gives you a balance between work and play. The contact you have with colleagues is an important thing you may need to replace in some form. You might feel you will be missing out on this camaraderie. It is important to think about, and plan ahead for, whether you want to leave it all behind or foster relationships for the future. Would you want to foster social relationships only or commercial ones too?

> Ask yourself: Do you think you'd want to leave work behind or continue to keep in touch? Can you think of particular colleagues you wish to maintain a relationship with? What do you think would be the best way to keep in touch with these people? For example, do you have shared interests/hobbies, do you live in close proximity to one and another?

It is psychologically "healthy" to have a leaving do, for you and for those saying goodbye. Farewell parties can be seen as a very stressful event, but they are actually important for closure; however, it is not imperative that you have one if you really can't face it!

Plan how you want to be remembered, if appropriate. Is there a legacy?

There is also an existential component to retirement that is worth considering: What have you achieved? What is your legacy? What is the meaning of your life?

> Ask yourself: How would you feel if you left work now?

How to retire from self-employment

It can be difficult to retire from self-employment, for a variety of reasons, such as:

- You have spent a long time building up the business and don't want to let it go.
- There is always one more project in the pipeline so the time is never right.
- You are not confident in the income your pension will give.
- You have been so immersed in the business that you don't have much of a life outside it.
- You are your business, so are unsure of your identity without it.
- You simply enjoy it too much to stop.

There are solutions, though. The obvious one is to reduce your hours, so you work less hard, and giving you more time to do other things. You could cherry-pick the work you undertake; alternatively, you could delegate anything you'd rather not do, or that could easily be done by someone else. In addition, you could look into having the business valued – investing the money you receive when you sell the business could give you a replacement income.

The hardest thing to do when you work for yourself is to take time to stop and think. Building an "exit" strategy into your business from an early stage means you have a plan for the future, a blueprint to follow. Of course, your next phase might be to set up another business! You can do whatever you want.

Consider this case example.

Monica, an entrepreneur, was thirty-eight when she made her first £22 million following the sale of her online business, which she had started on her own, twelve years before. Coming from a modest background and with no financial help from anyone in her family, she literally built the business up herself and, through a combination of incredibly hard work, hiring the right people, good fortune and having a keen sense as an entrepreneur, she was able to realise her success. Unlike some other successful people she met in the context of her work, she had never intended to retire at such an early age and felt conflicted by the good fortune that she now enjoyed. She realised that being wealthy meant she could do pretty much whatever she wanted and she would never have to work again.

However, not long after the dust had settled from the windfall coming into her bank account, Monica realised that what she really needed and wanted in life was actually quite modest. She certainly did not feel a need to spend it all, although she was, by her own standards, generous with those who had supported her throughout her career to date.

A further challenge emerged. Her partner Richard, a PT teacher in a local primary school, also found himself thrust into a new situation in which he too did not have to work. It was never part of his "life script" or ambition to retire at such an early age and, although his salary was modest in relation to Monica's own wealth, Richard felt passionately about the work that he did and wanted to continue being a PT teacher for the foreseeable future.

Wisely, Monica and Richard realised the necessity of sitting down and planning how they would manage their wealth, their lives and their relationship, rather than letting their newfound wealth dictate the terms. Having no experience in similar matters and no mental or life coach to help them through this challenge, they decided that it was in Richard's best interest to continue in his job for the foreseeable future. Monica, in contrast, felt there were a number of health and hobby interests that she wanted to take up in the next six months. These included raising her standard of fitness and stamina as a long-distance cyclist, learning pottery and also completing a short course on philanthropy.

There was a small risk that the couple would grow apart as Richard continued to pursue his PT job and Monica branched out to fulfil her needs and interests outside of a regular working context. Within a few months, however, Monica recognised that she needed to engage her entrepreneurial and leadership skills more. What had felt like a six-month temporary retirement came to an end when she and a friend set up a charity for raising the standards of training and equipment available for PT training in Africa. This combined Richard's interests and career aspirations with her own, and he contributed with this new enterprise. Monica is now five years into her second career and, having taken a short retirement break, is back at work – although a different kind to the one she previously enjoyed. It seems apparent from what Monica feels and has expressed that she sees her life as comprising a series of intense work episodes followed by small periods of retirement where she is able to switch off and follow her own patterns and needs, while she regroups and comes up with new ideas for her future.

How to retire from unemployment

You might not actually be working at the time you reach your official "retirement" age. However, this provides you with a focal point at which you can implement long-held dreams or plans. It might just be the impetus you need to take control, rather than simply carrying on as before.

If you were job-hunting, there is no longer any need; and if you weren't, then there's no need to do so ever again! That phase of your life is past, and it's up to you what you make of the next phase.

What next?

The core theme of this book is that your retirement is not the end of things. There is life after retirement, and you are the one who can decide what to do with it! There are many choices in the new, post-retirement phase, known as "unretirement", and they are all exciting.

So, if you don't want to carry on as before, or are perhaps unable to do so, you need to decide what you do want to do. Of course, if you've planned ahead you will know what you want to do next. Otherwise, remember you don't have to decide straight away: engaging in something purposeful for a minimum of 5 hours per week will help you adjust, so, in addition to those in the previous chapter, here are some ideas for you to consider.

Carry on working

The latest available figures from the Office of National Statistics in 2017 showed that more people than ever aged 50+ are working, and there are now more than a million workers aged 65+. Every year more than 10 per cent more of us are working past retirement age. It is now no longer expected that retirement means stopping work. The word "retirement" these days seems to signify only the point at which you are eligible for the state pension, and even that is currently being revised upwards to save the government the cost of funding an ageing population.

In fact, 24 per cent of people likely to retire in 2013 said they were not ready to stop work. More than 20 per cent didn't like the idea of being stuck at home after retirement.

Setting up on your own

If you have always worked for someone else, retirement might be the perfect time to start up a business. There's a lot of help and support out there, and a growing number of people are setting up on their own. According to the *Huffington Post*, there are now record numbers, accounting for 96 per cent of the UK private sector and about a third of private sector turnover. Small businesses are now a major force in the UK economy.

In July 2018 there were 300,000 unemployed people aged 50–64, over a quarter of whom have been unemployed for more than a year. What a waste of expertise!

Prince Charles set up the Prince's Initiative for Mature Enterprise (PRIME; www.prime.org.uk) in 1999, along the lines of his Prince's Trust, but instead for people aged 50+ who are out of work or facing redundancy to prepare for self-employment and enterprise. PRIME is now part of the charity Business in the Community to harness the "missing million" older workers who have been involuntarily pushed out of the workforce. This could boost the UK economy by £88 billion. Stephen Howard, Chief Executive of Business in the Community, said: "There are a significant number of over 50s who would be willing to work if the right opportunity arose but we are failing to harness their potential."

Beware the traps

It is easy to think you can do all sorts of things when you are no longer working, but most "retirees" say they have never been so busy and wonder how they ever managed to fit work in as well! Others may see you as "fair game" to help out themselves or their cause in a variety of ways. To avoid being overwhelmed, it is important not to take on too much ... and learn to say "no".

The volunteering trap

Volunteering can be a wonderful thing to do. However, a lot is done by a few (a cynic might say it is usually the same few), and it can be hard to resist when there is so much need. As soon as it becomes known that you might have some time free, you will be asked to get involved in all sorts of worthy organisations! Choose wisely – you must put yourself and your own needs first, and remember to keep a balance in your life.

The failing to fly the nest trap

Do you want to be a hands-on parent for ever? These days it can be hard to push your chicks out of the nest. Over a million and a half adults aged 20–40 are living at home because they cannot afford to move out. And before you agree to an adult child returning to the family home, consider that this will add nearly £850 a year to your household bills. You might be delighted they want to be with you, but equally you might not, which can lead to friction, disagreement and stress.

To minimise potential difficulties, agree ground rules regarding help with bills, food and cooking, laundry, visitors and so on. They are grown up, after all.

The caring trap

It is not always possible to say no to caring for others, and of course you might not want to do so, but it is important to ask for help and support, and protect your own health and financial position. Explore alternative options if you can't cope. Taking care of others might not be something we feel much choice over. Choosing to care for someone is obviously the best context or scenario as our motivation, genuine sense of caring and affiliation and possibly our availability are likely to have been considered and planned for.

Two further scenarios present more complexity and challenge. The first is having to care for someone else, because it is "expected", a "duty", there is no one else to do it or other options for care are unaffordable. In such instances, there is a sense of conflict or duality. Caring interferes with or disrupts what we want to do, but we don't feel naturally inclined. This can lead to resentment, irritability, transactional caring (characterised by helping to do the task, but the process lacking any empathy, sensitivity or emotional warmth). Some carers in this situation may find that if they do not find healthy activities for themselves to switch off and look after themselves, they may be at greater risk of unhealthy behaviours such as excessive alcohol use or Internet addiction. Respite care may be a necessary and welcome relief. All carers – whether family or professional – need to take care of themselves and receive care for themselves.

The second scenario is caring for one's loved one. While few of us in long-term relationships really thought deeply about the implications of a commitment "in sickness and in health", caring for a loved one can be challenging and at times painfully and seemingly impossibly hard. Again, we may have conflicted feelings with role changes, increasing dependency, loss of physical and mental activity, the limiting of our own lives, and the intrusion of healthcare professionals into our lives. We may also fear loss and being on our own in the future, with no one to take care of us.

These reactions and fears are of course normal; however, without further support such as from other family members, neighbours, GP and a counsellor, this most sensitive of caring roles can become overwhelmingly burdensome and fraught.

Many newly retired people, especially women, can end up working harder than they ever did in a job! They become carers, not only for grandchildren, so their child or children can go to work, but also for their parents. They then become trapped between a rock and a hard place, as part of the so-called "sandwich" generation. Research by the Money Advice Service shows 4.7 million adults (10 per cent of the UK adult population) are currently sandwich carers, and a third of them are struggling to cope with basic living costs. This number is expected to continue to rise, as our population ages and care costs rise. The Money Advice Service can offer support to those in dual-carer roles.

One in ten of us is caring for older or disabled family members, according to the Office of National Statistics figures from the 2011 Census. The number of people caring for our sick, disabled or elderly loved ones without pay continues to rise, with 4 million people providing up to 19 hours of care a week, and more than 1.5 million caring for more than 50 hours a week without pay (ONS official labour market statistics from 2011 Census).

All of this can take a toll on our health, so in the next chapter we take a look at ways to be healthier as we age.

Chapter 8

Mind your health

Oliver Patrick

Quick fix for successful ageing

Let me start with the actions. If you want to avoid the hassle of reading the entire chapter, please do just implement the five actions below and you can expect a significant and long-lasting impact on your health, wellbeing and longevity:

- Keep moving.
- Do strength training.
- Eat a Mediterranean diet.
- Keep mentally stimulated.
- Keep track of your function for early changes.

It is an interesting, and at times difficult, process assisting people with their lifestyle choices. Of all the stages of life I have had the fortune of coaching my clients through, perhaps retirement offers the most complex set of opportunities and risks. Over the last nearly two decades I have gained a unique insight into what is often perceived to be a golden period of our lives. I, like most people I know, spend hours gazing at my dust-covered golf clubs, longing for a stage in life when time is my own again and my daily to do list is full of hobbies and fun filled activities – a sequence of long held wishes being ticked off in turn. This is retirement.

However, the reality of what many believe about retirement rarely considers the impact of worsening health and the benefits the working environment brought to keep health and wellbeing in place.

The role that allows me access to the intimate details of people at all stages of life is that of a private client health manager. In a nutshell, I use my physiologist background to oversee all facets of my clients – those fortunate to be able to afford the services of myself and our company. I note my role, as it is important to the context of the following insights into retirement and healthy ageing. My experience gives me an insight based on people rather than on academic journals and theory. I have spent many hundreds of hours speaking with people of all stages of life about the most interesting of topics – their health, their wellbeing and their happiness.

My thoughts are based on a unique insight into the thinking of the working – and well – population, and it has been a great blessing to have been able to follow individual clients over many years and see their journey through health, mapped against their journey through life.

The science to my recommendations is robust and strong; however, the science is not important, the actions you take are all that matter. The thoughts I share in this chapter are not from the textbook but instead are "principles" to follow based on thousands of case studies, above and beyond the textbooks' opinion of what might/should/ could happen to health. If you follow these thoughts to a positive lifestyle change I can almost guarantee a better future for you and those around you. The personal cost of implementing new actions at this stage of life is something I cannot help you with, as much as I wish I could.

Move

Wearable technology has been the success story of the last few years. Apple's Watch is the icing on a cake that includes devices to measure everything from your blood sugar and cholesterol up to when you are getting a cold or flu by how much you use your phone. However, the base for all these technologies is the humble pedometer, and with the pedometer comes perhaps the most valuable "traceable" figure: movement.

Are you moving enough? The fact is you were designed to move – and regularly. If you move only a little your body will lose the ability to move. It is really that simple. I am going to talk about exercise in a moment, but first I want to distinguish that from moving – they are not the same thing. If you are not walking between 8000 and 10,000 steps a day, you cannot expect the same healthy future as someone who is. At this point I am aware of the frustrations of those with arthritis, those with musculoskeletal restrictions, those who can't move – my apologies for what feels like an exclusion piece of advice but, as with all thoughts in this chapter, I have to target the majority without the caveats and alternatives for the minority. Move it or lose it. And it doesn't count as exercise, it counts as activity – a different thing.

Exercise

Many people use their walking as the key focus of discussions around movement, exercise and fitness. It is great that you walk; however, let's distinguish carefully between walking – which your body should be doing at all times – and exercise that stresses your body to strengthen and develop. They are quite different things.

Let me start this section with a difficult to position caveat. That caveat is I don't care if you feel you are an exception to what I am saying. It is very likely you are not and I will explain such a bold statement.

Health messaging is a very difficult message to get across in a contextual and inclusive fashion, yet without being personalised to the individual reader it seems to be irrelevant and ignorable. At every health talk I deliver or in many one-on-one discussions around health I will hear the following phrases:

- Smoking cessation: "Well, I know someone who smoked a pack a day and lived to be 100."
- Weight management: "I don't eat a thing and I still gain weight."
- Sleep cycles: "I don't get affected by caffeine at all – I can drink it and fall straight to sleep."
- Exercise modality: "Running is bad for my knees."

With the advent of social media and instant, accessible feedback it is clear that general health messaging has become confusing. People are more interested in proving how they are the exception to health rules rather than believing they could be part of the majority. Often, through the inclusion of the voice of the exception alongside the "headline news" being promoted, we are faced with confusing and contradictory messaging.

Diminishing muscle mass

Ageing is a complex process, but there is one thing we know for sure: as you age you lose muscle mass. We know this when we look at an ageing human we often see the following patterns develop:

- small/wasted muscles;
- a forwards/hunched posture;
- lacking strength and unable to lift heavy items; and
- poor ability to generate quick/dynamic movement – like jumping.

An interesting question is: are these observations features of ageing or, as an alternative opinion, do these changes perhaps cause ageing? In my experience it is the latter – these features cause ageing, and as such this pattern can be significantly delayed – if not avoided completely.

If the loss of muscle mass causes the issues above and these issues feed issues of "ageing" then it is sensible we should try to understand why muscle mass decreases as we age and what we can do to stop it. This is fundamental to successful ageing.

Muscle mass is brilliant; we call it active tissue because it is always working. Muscle mass/volume is the key feature in how many calories we burn each day because each kilogram of muscle burns calories even when you are not moving. Keeping active tissue like muscle depends on two things:

1   The right hormonal environment to sustain muscle mass.
2   The right stimulus to ensure the body sustains muscle mass.

This book is not the correct place to go into the complexities of managing hormones in ageing and treating this, so I am going to focus on the second point: the right stimulus to sustain muscle mass.

The reality of muscle mass loss – called muscle atrophy – is that it is a battle we all face at some point in our lives. It is also a key contributor to the progressive and frustrating weight gain referred to as the "middle aged spread". Being such a high energy demanding tissue means the body is very keen to keep muscle volume to a minimum. This is because burning calories takes a toll on the body, much like mileage takes a toll on a car's components. As the body moves through its thirties into later life, the body's desire to drop muscle is really the key element in what people refer to as the middle-aged spread.

In muscle mass and the gradual loss of muscle mass we can actually see many of the problems of ageing. Muscle mass has a role in:

- sustaining metabolic rate – managing your weight and energy
- securing your skeleton – controlling your posture and avoidance of back pain
- managing blood glucose – avoidance of diabetes.
- And, of course, the vital importance of muscle mass is that it enables people to exercise!

So, what's the solution?

Believe it or not, the answer is weight training, or resistance exercise if we wish to be more technically correct. We need the ageing, retired population to join the gym, to buy the weights bench, to pump some iron. Man, woman, centenarian – one and all.

Of course, any good physiologist will look at fitness in a broad sense. There are many different forms of fitness and each has its own benefits to health and the weighting of those benefits will depend on the individual in question. For example, of the five key areas of fitness – strength, stamina, speed, suppleness and skill – each may be the priority area of focus depending on the context of the individual. Examples of this could be:

- Strength – priority area for someone trying to lose weight.
- Stamina – priority area for someone with high risk of heart disease.
- Speed – priority area for someone still trying to play competitive sport (e.g. tennis).
- Suppleness/flexibility – priority area for someone suffering from pain due to imbalanced muscles.
- Skill – priority area for someone recovering from a stroke and learning to walk again.

Knowing which area of fitness is most applicable to you is vital, as working one does not necessarily precipitate benefit in the other. I hear many clients who come to me saying they are "fit" because they walk each day, or they are "fit" because they do Pilates each week. I sadly have to let them know they may be fit – but perhaps not in the area of "fitness" their body most needs.

> Ask yourself: What is my priority area for fitness? What areas of my fitness am I willing to improve?

The message underlying this is each individual may have a greater, specific need for an area of fitness but all people who are ageing – therefore all people – need strength to keep muscle mass and to slow the pathway of normal ageing.

For those looking for the actual solution I will paint a basic picture. You need your key muscle groups to each perform weights twice each week. The Harvard School of Public Health showed that 20 minutes of weight training had a greater benefit for abdominal fat loss and muscle mass than an equivalent 20 minutes spent on cardiovascular work. That study was of 11,000 men over 40 years old, but it matches with everything I see day in day out with both male and female clients. You need to do that 20 minutes at least twice, ideally three times, each week. Otherwise, don't expect the benefits noted.

Second on the list of "fitness" areas to be aware of we have an even tie. There is a huge number of studies showing the health benefit of aerobic and cardiovascular exercise on limiting the impact of heart disease and stroke. This is fact. However, the reason cardiovascular disease is not a straight choice for my second key area of fitness is this. You need to be fit enough to do it.

So often in health consultations we hear sentences such as "I used to play tennis before my knees gave way" or "I can't run anymore because of my back". There is no point dwelling on what you would like to do or used to do, the skill is to overcome the reasons you cannot do. If you can't move, you can't benefit from the same physiology as someone who can. Movement is the soil from which strength and stamina grow, keeping coordination, keeping balance, keeping ageing at bay.

People tend to become more sedentary during retirement. When people are distressed, fearful and so on, physical exertion is one of the great antidotes. The act of doing exercises releases endorphins which lift your mood and suppresses releases of cortisol, which is released in to the blood when we feel stressed.

Your main goal should be to look after yourself physically and remain socially active.

> Ask yourself: How could you start to be as active as your parents and grandparents were, with a view to improving your health for the future?

To make sure you keep physically active, here are some more great ideas:

- Run. The Copenhagen City Heart Study revealed that runners typically live around 6 years longer than non-runners. Regular cardiovascular workouts reduce the risk of cancer and heart disease. Alternating sprinting with walking or jogging, known as interval training, is better for you and you'll burn more calories.
- Dance. If you don't like the idea of running or the gym, dancing three times a week has been shown by the Albert Einstein College of Medicine to be good for reducing the risk of high blood pressure, type II diabetes and cardiovascular disease.
- Walk. A metastudy conducted by the *Journal of Clinical Practice* reported that walking for only 20 minutes a day could save 37,000 lives a year, and can help you beat up to 24 illnesses.

- Have sex. Research by the *British Medical Journal* found that men who orgasm three times a week halve their risk of dying from coronary heart disease. Similarly, the US Longevity Project found that women who orgasm regularly also live longer. This is due to endorphins, which not only make you feel better but also help neutralise stress hormones, which are responsible for a variety of diseases such as cancer and heart disease.
- Sing out. Singing is a surprisingly good all-round exercise for the muscles and organs of the upper body, and reduces stress. It is also a sociable activity and therefore good for you according to a joint study by Harvard and Yale universities.
- Shop more. Yes, really! The National Health Research Institutes of Taiwan found that those who shop more often than once a week are 27 per cent less likely to die over a ten-year period than those who only shop weekly. This makes sense when you consider the distance walked, bags carried and conversations held in the average shopping trip.

> Ask yourself: What can I do to improve my fitness?

When looking at the heart and cardiovascular system we have an almost endless array of tests, scans and evaluations to gauge its health, and its risk of impending disease. And while it is true that cardiovascular disease and stroke are the biggest killers in the UK, and much of the western world, it always seems a strange volume of testing compared with another important health system: the brain.

Brain function

> Anyone who stops learning is old, whether at twenty or eighty. Anyone who keeps learning stays young. The greatest thing in life is to keep your mind young.
>
> Henry Ford

The brain is a notoriously complex organ. The most calorie-demanding organ in the body is also the least understood. What we do know is that disease of the brain and decline of the brain are important areas to try to prevent, despite a lack of critical tests and processes to gauge improvements.

Over 500,000 people in the UK have Alzheimer's disease, with an incidence close to 1 in 4 in those over 85. However, it has been shown that people over 60 engaging in mentally challenging activities once per week have a 7 per cent less risk of dementia over a 20-year period. That is a crucial finding and gives an indication to the rise in cognitive "games" testing brain power and the like. Of these, Lumosity (www.lumosity.com) seems to be the market leader, but the sector will grow and your iPad, iPhone, laptop or similar is well placed to test your brain on a daily basis.

When people say retirement is one of the most dangerous things you can do, they are often thinking of the brain rather than the heart. Most jobs and daily office work tasks the brain with dynamic problem solving, complex social engagement, logistical planning, mathematics etc. Much like a bodybuilder suddenly stopping weights and expecting to keep muscle, a retiring professional must be wary of the message being passed to brain tissue.

The brain is not a muscle, but it does seem to follow some of the general rules of physiology – similar to that of muscle tissue. What is used regularly will remain. In the same way that the muscles must remain stimulated, the coordination and balance response regularly tested and the heart overloaded, the brain must be tested and asked to "stay". At present the science is behind the theory, but cognitive reserve goes some way to show that a well-used brain is more robust in the face of progressive damage of the sort Alzheimer's causes all too often.

Food

Nutritional advice over the past few years has become more complex than is worthwhile. I used to firmly believe there was an education gap in healthy living that was a root cause in many issues seen in our medical clinic. I still believe this but instead of a lack of education it is a lack of clarity around which health message is relevant. Which message is robust and which is worth implementing, often at great personal discomfort, for example strength training.

To avoid trying to personalise this small section of eating, I will cover the key principles that are non-negotiable. Retirement offers the first opportunity in many years to break behaviours, look at things with a fresh perspective and eating and eating well will bring benefits far beyond the obvious cosmetic and body composition changes.

Mediterranean diet

The National Institute for Health found a startling 34 per cent reduction in Alzheimer's for those with the highest adherence to a Mediterranean-style diet compared with those with the lowest adherence to the same style of eating.

Eating as those living around the Mediterranean Sea have traditionally done involves the following:

- Maximising your intake of vegetables, peas and beans (legumes), fruits and wholegrain cereals.
- Eating fish and poultry as your primary meats – keeping red meat to a minimum.
- Using mono-saturated, liquid fats like olive oil, instead of hard and saturated fats.
- Limiting your intake of processed foods. Avoid anything you did not make or see made from scratch.
- Snacking on nuts, vegetables and fruit – but ideally fruit with nuts rather than on its own.
- Limiting dairy produce as much as possible.
- Not adding salt to your food after cooking.
- Drinking red wine, but no more than three small glasses per day if you are a man and no more than two small glasses per day if you are a woman.
- Limiting all beverages that are not water or herbal teas. Certainly no diet drinks or processed drinks.

The Mediterranean diet should be backed up with the following three simple principles that should always be borne in mind in all eating decision making:

- balance your blood sugar;
- nourish yourself; and
- eat mindfully.

Ask yourself: How good is your diet, really? What improvements could you make?

Balance your blood sugar

Ageing and insulin do not mix well. Avoid producing insulin and avoid sugar spikes by restricting refined carbohydrate, sugar and sweet foods to an absolute minimum. Ahead of restricting fat intake, this is the key to good living.

Nourish yourself

On testing the nutrient status of clients, we find a very similar pattern in all of our retiring male and females. The pattern is such:

- low vitamin D;
- low B vitamins;
- high omega 6 fats – indicating excessive processed foods;
- low omega 3 fat – indicating insufficient oily fish;
- low digestive bacteria – indicating regular use of antibiotics;
- low magnesium – indicating a lack of unrefined foods/grains in particular; and
- low CoQ10.

It is almost impossible to influence diet sufficiently to target micronutrient groups like those noted above. The reality is people don't shop or eat against an internal list of viable and less viable food groups.

As such, despite the uncertainty around taking pills, low dosage supplements are a sensible approach to maximise nutrient levels of these elements. Supplements are broadly unproven, but work on a sound logic of "supplementing" areas of diet that are either deficient in intake or are required in excessive amounts by the body.

Food state nutrients are a safer "toe in the water" with starting supplements, as they are made like food and have a better absorption and uptake (early studies suggest) than their chemically manufactured counterparts. You can find these online if you are keen to explore further. When I see clients before and after they are taking supplements I can measure notable positive differences in the results and in their appearance, symptoms, energy and so on.

Eat mindfully

Eating slowly, respecting food, creating meals from scratch. All these habits bring benefit beyond the obvious trait of fewer spillages down shirts or an upset tummy from being too full. Digestion is an ever-growing area of focus in health. Digestion and sleep will be the big areas for focus in future years as our understanding of the gut's role in general health grows with new findings.

Track yourself

The body is a series of systems. Track your systems functioning and control the point at which a positive and potentially lifesaving "intervention" can be made.

There is no perfect heath check or a series of examinations I could suggest that would suit each person. However, lifestyle disease, unlike infectious disease, does not arise overnight and can build gently over decades. Tracking yourself, putting numbers against your functions, can be a vital aide in guiding you and your health professionals to early and potentially sinister change.

Table 8.1 shows some of the clinical features we track in our health evaluation for our clients. The second column, however, reflects something that can be easily tracked at home to give a similar picture that may offer a similar insight to negative changes in the body. These metrics are worth tracking in a personal way to note if something may be changing in your body and cause you to gather a medical opinion on how best to manage at an early stage.

Table 8.1 Clinically observed features and how to track them at home

Clinical	Home
Segmental body composition analysis	Measure home body composition
Cardiovascular risk factors	Monitor fat and sugar intake
Aerobic fitness measurement	Recovery heart rate
Tracking inflammatory factors	Look at skin quality and dryness
Musculoskeletal evaluation	Leg squats and push ups
Cognition and memory tests	Use an online tool (e.g. Lumosity)
Neurophysiology markers	Mood diary, journaling
Sleep analysis recovery and quality	Check your heart rate first thing in the morning
Measurement of nourishment	Quality nutrition/supplementation
Monitor digestive function	Food diaries and probiotics
Measure immune function	Keep an eye on colds/ill health – boost immune elements

Ask yourself: Which of these health markers could you track?

Retirement as an opportunity to improve your health

Science to drive action has limited impact; in my opinion, books to drive behaviours have little impact – I hope that is not the case here but I suspect it may be. I only write this chapter in the hope that you do make one or more small changes and that change has a significant difference on your retirement and life long beyond retirement.

In summary, bear in mind the five key points emphasised at the head of this chapter. Also, here are some more ideas for improving your mental and physical wellbeing for successful ageing:

- Be creative. The *Journal of Aging and Health* found that being creative can increase your longevity by up to 12 per cent. By trying new things, you are increasing the neural pathway in your brain. Take up an activity you enjoyed in your youth or try something new!
- Be positive. If you want to live 19 per cent longer than negative people, start being positive! Count your blessings, keep a journal of things you are grateful for, say thank you more, complement others more, use positive language, and hold your head up high. Avoid moaning, avoid putting people down and avoid complaining. Life would be so much better for you and those around you!
- Be curious. The Centre for Health Sciences at SRI International discovered that those interested in the world around them are less stressed and healthier. Be interested in others, ask people questions about themselves, engage with others, interact on social media.
- Stroke the dog. Queen's University Belfast has found that dog owners have lower blood pressure and fewer medical problems than others, as stroking a pet reduces your heart rate and the levels of stress hormones.

As well as a healthy mind and body, it is important for your future that you have a healthy bank account too. We investigate how to plan for this in the next chapter.

Chapter 9

Mind your money

Financial planning for retirement

Martin Jones and Waterson Jones

Preparing for retirement financially is about building up enough assets/income sources to meet your financial objectives when you stop working. In reality, it is rarely so straightforward. There are other financial pressures such as paying for somewhere to live, funding your children's education or paying back the loans to fund yours! Financial objectives will range from the ideal (never having to worry all the way to the grave) to the reluctant compromise. Stopping work may be a gradual process rather than an abrupt end. Life is unpredictable but this is one area where you can leave it too late and it is sensible to devise a plan now accepting that it will have to be reviewed as circumstances and the wider financial environment change.

The need for individuals to take control of their retirement planning is a relatively recent development. For many years, most people would have had little if any capacity to save and life expectancy was low. During the twentieth century the picture changed, with the state and employers providing comparatively generous pension provision. The self-employed could rely on good investment returns and high annuity rates for their pension savings. Unfortunately, the outlook for many has deteriorated in this century. In the private sector, generous employer pensions schemes, typically provided via final salary arrangements where the employer took on the longevity and investment risks, have been closed to new joiners although many public-sector workers continue to benefit. Pensions for many employees now resemble self-employed arrangements where individuals are exposed to investment returns and annuity rates. Investment returns have deteriorated with the FT100 Index for shares at August 2018 barely different to its level at the end of 1999. Annuity rates have collapsed following the financial crisis as policy makers slashed interest rates to historic lows.

The state still provides a basic pension, but this is at the level of subsistence. Recent reforms compel all employers to provide and contribute to company pension schemes but these are not final salary arrangements and the risks fall on the members rather than the employer. Planning has been further complicated by the high cost of housing, which reduces the amount available for retirement savings. Increasingly, the pressure is on individuals to take retirement planning in to their own hands.

How much income will you need?

The first step in financial planning for retirement is to estimate spending. This is hard enough to do without worrying about inflation, so it makes sense to ignore cost of living increases and to cater for inflation when planning investment returns (i.e. to assume returns net of inflation, referred to as "real" returns). In other words, how much would you need to meet annual living expenses if you retired tomorrow? Arguably, the default position should assume mortgage and other debts have been repaid and children are no longer dependent, with appropriate adjustments where this may not be the case. The amount of detail will depend on how far you are from retirement and how much you enjoy this kind of exercise. Simply adding up the total debits from your current account in a 12-month period is not a bad start. It is more difficult to estimate the annual equivalent costs of large occasional items, such as house maintenance and car purchase, but it is essential to take these into account. It might seem reasonable to allow for falling expenses over time, with the assumption that the early postretirement years will be taken up with exotic and expensive travel whereas in later years you might settle for a comfy chair and a crossword, but this could be wishful thinking with other expenses such as health and personal care replacing travel.

> Ask yourself: How much income will I need?

How much capital will you need?

The next step is to compare expected income sources in retirement with expenses and to capitalise any shortfall, that is to work out how much capital you need to generate the extra income. Income sources for this purpose are income payments where you have no or little control over the capital, such as pensions from the State and your employer.

The basic state pension is available to individuals with a sufficient record of National Insurance contributions. In 2018/19, it is £164.35 per week (£8546.20 per annum). There is a formula to increase the pension to provide protection from rising prices. The pension is taxable. The state pension age (SPA) is currently 65 for men. It was lower for women; however, the SPA is scheduled to increase and will be equalised for men and women by late 2018 and will then increase in increments for all to 68 by 2039.

Employer sponsored pension schemes are common, particularly among larger companies. Typically, schemes are either final salary (defined benefit) or money purchase (defined contribution). Final salary schemes pay an income in retirement dependent on earnings and length of service. In these schemes it is the employer who bears the risks. Money purchase schemes pay an income which depends on the amount of savings accumulated in the scheme. They are essentially a form of personal pension where the risks lie with the employee rather than the employer.

Recently, legislation has been introduced to compel employers and employees to contribute to company pension schemes. Minimum contributions will be required. These are a percentage of qualifying earnings and will increase over time to 8 per cent of which the employer must contribute at least 3 per cent. Employer pension contributions are a real tangible financial benefit and employees who are in a scheme where employers will "match" higher voluntary contributions paid by employees should give these serious consideration as there is often no alternative compensation.

It is important to understand the amounts of your current and projected entitlements to State and company pensions. A lucky few may find that existing or projected income sources are sufficient to meet living expenses in retirement without the need to accumulate other savings. This is more likely for long-standing members of final salary schemes.

An important feature of financial planning for retirement is that "income" has a different meaning in this context. In particular, retirement income refers to payments received, which may comprise of original capital and/or income generated by investing the capital and/or capital gains generated by investing the capital. It does not refer solely to the income derived from investing capital. Unless you have very substantial sums indeed, it is impossible to survive on investment income alone and if you could then you should arguably be looking at making gifts to reduce the potential Inheritance Tax on death.

It is impossible to work out how much capital you might need without predicting the date of your demise (obviously there is no need for income after that point) and this is where annuities come in to their own.

Ask yourself: How much capital will I need?

Annuities

Annuities are issued by insurance companies and typically guarantee an income for life in return for a capital sum. In effect, they insure you against the risk of living too long. Annuity rates are a good indication of capital required, for example if the rate is 5 per cent and, ignoring taxation, you need income of £20,000 per annum then you will require a capital sum of £400,000. Annuities have had a very poor press in recent years as rates have slumped, meaning that more capital is required to buy the same income, but this is largely a function of low interest rates, themselves a result of deliberate government/central bank policy. There are ready alternatives to annuities, but the main feature is that they involve a "do it yourself" approach – you must decide when you think you will die and what the investment return will be in the meantime. Underestimating the former and/or overestimating the latter will leave you short during your lifetime.

Whether you choose to buy an annuity (there is no longer any compulsion to do this with pension savings) will depend on personal circumstances and preferences; however, it is a very useful technique to find out the annuity rate and extrapolate from this the amount of capital you require. You can then decide whether to buy an annuity or make different investments with some comfort that your calculation is on solid ground.

What return do you need?

Once the capital required has been established, it is possible to calculate the annual average real rate of investment return necessary on current and future anticipated savings in order to achieve the target capital by retirement date. In theory, this should drive the key investment decision, which is how to apportion savings between the different asset classes. The main asset classes are cash, fixed-interest (e.g. gilts and corporate bonds), inflation-linked, equities (shares), commercial and residential property, and commodities, and asset allocation refers to how you distribute savings between these. In theory, asset allocation should be driven by the rate of return required: If the rate can be achieved from lower risk investments (broadly speaking, the first three categories above) then there should be no reason to buy higher risk ones.

For younger savers in particular, the average rate required may be higher than can be achieved on lower risk investments and potentially even greater than can be achieved on higher risk assets. Leaving personal attitudes to risk to one side, the maths may suggest the only hope of succeeding is to invest entirely in higher risk investments such as equities (shares). However, as you get older and savings accumulate you may find that the required return reduces over time and it becomes possible to switch some savings to lower risk investments. Ideally, if you reach a stage where your objectives could be achieved by investing entirely in lower risk assets you should consider switching everything to these in case subsequent losses change the position.

UK government index-linked (inflation-linked) gilts offer capital protection in nominal terms (because of the credit worthiness of government) and in real terms, that is they are guaranteed to keep pace with inflation. For many years, the real return which is the return above inflation hovered around 2 per cent per annum; however, increased demand since the financial crisis has seen prices increase so that returns to new buyers are now around nil in real terms or even less than nil where the gilt matures in the short term.

Other than living too long, the greatest risks are arguably loss of capital and inflation, and in that sense index-linked gilts ought to be the benchmark against which all other investments are measured. If you require a higher return than can be provided by these, you will need to take risk. Equities (shares) are the most popular higher risk asset class. Apart from the obvious risk of losing money, there is a particular risk in retirement planning and it applies to the postretirement period when you may be withdrawing money from savings to meet income requirements. Most projections of equity returns assume a steady rate over time. In fact, returns can be highly volatile. This means that a plan that worked assuming an annual return of say 5 per cent might never work if the early returns are significantly negative and you have no alternative but to continue to make withdrawals to meet living expenses. Unless you can postpone withdrawals until markets recover, the recalibrated average annual return required for the plan to work after an early setback could be so high that there is little realistic chance of success.

It is important to distinguish between underlying assets and the vehicles used to acquire and hold these. Pensions and individual savings accounts (ISAs) do not generate investment returns. Rather, they are "shells" to accommodate investments. The returns will depend largely on what you choose to buy within the shell. The particular advantages of these vehicles are tax-driven. In particular, investment returns are largely exempt from income and capital gains tax.

Ask yourself: When will I start planning financially for my retirement?

Tax relief and legislation

Pensions have some additional tax advantages in that contributions up to a maximum (the annual allowance, currently £40,000) can be relieved against income tax. When money is withdrawn from pensions (referred to as benefits), it is generally possible to take some as a tax-free lump sum. However, the rest of the fund will be taxed like earned income in the tax year(s) when it is withdrawn. HMRC make no distinction between original capital invested, investment income, or capital gains. All benefits beyond tax-free cash are liable to income tax.

ISAs do not attract tax relief on contributions (the maximum is currently £20,000 per person per tax year); however, there is no tax to pay at any stage in the future. Also, it is possible to withdraw money from ISA at any time without notice or penalty. Pension benefits are only available from age 55. Both pensions and ISAs have valuable roles to play in financial planning for retirement. Arguably, it is easier to overstate the advantages of pensions, but the attraction of employers' contributions, where these are available, may make pensions the first choice.

Pension legislation was "simplified" in 2006, since when it has become increasingly more complex. Austerity measures have drastically cut back the amount of contributions attracting tax relief and larger funds, in excess of the lifetime allowance (now £1,030,000), are exposed to an additional tax charge on the excess. That said the most recent change has the potential to genuinely simplify. From April 2015, legislation permitted pension benefits to be withdrawn any time, in whole or in part, from age 55 without restrictions.

Money in bricks

In an economy obsessed with house prices it would be unrealistic to ignore the potential for residential property to contribute to financial planning for retirement. There is no tax relief on investment save that main residences are free of capital gains tax and buy-to-let mortgage interest can be relieved against rental income. You cannot buy within a pension or an ISA. Property is also inflexible insofar as you cannot rely on selling when you most need to sell or easily dispose of portions of a house.

The potential role of property stems from the very large amounts of wealth tied up this way. Younger savers should not look a gift horse in the mouth, so an element of pension savings, if only to ensure employer contributions, will be attractive. Bearing in mind maximum pension savings have been severely curtailed by austerity legislation, it also makes sense to try to maximise ISAs. Beyond that, few will have sufficient savings to do more than try to achieve a roof over their heads.

The most straightforward solution is to downsize, that is to exchange a larger house for a smaller one, and use the capital released to fund living expenses. Alternatively, where you do not wish to move home, equity release arrangements allow you to borrow against the value of the house. There are various ways of doing this; for example, depending on the value of the house and your age, a financial institution may offer you a lump sum without requiring interest or capital repayment during your lifetime. Instead, interest is accumulated and repaid from the proceeds of selling the house, usually on death or on going into full-time care, if earlier. These types of arrangement will typically guarantee that you can continue to live in the house regardless of the future value of the debt or house.

Where residential property is taken into account in financial planning for retirement, the value should count towards the capital required to meet living expenses.

In this chapter, I have given a number of methods you can utilise to help plan for financial security in retirement. Only you know the best route for you, but planning and preparing, as with other aspects of retirement, are far more valuable than doing nothing.

Sticking to the serious stuff, it is important that you get your house in order, or at least your paperwork.

In the concluding chapter we bring together everything we have explored in this book and provide you with a blueprint for a healthy retirement i mind, body and wallet.

Chapter 10

Thoughts on life (after work)

Rosie Bank, network marketer

> We all go through stages in our lives and we cannot predict the future. But we can plan for it, and all of life's unexpected twists and turns.
>
> Are you planning for your future, especially the things that you cannot foresee?

Helen Mirren, actress

> You know, you have your dream of what it's going to be like to be retired. My husband and I have been building this house in Italy that's sort of our retirement dream, but in reality whether we ever will actually do that, I don't know.

Bette Davis, actress

> Getting old isn't for sissies.

Dame Jenni Murray, Radio 4's Women's Hour presenter

> I'd be happy to go with my headphones on.

Ruby Wax, TV interviewer

> Although it's scary to be getting older, worrying about it is the very thing that will kill you the quickest. An enlightened person is someone who can say, without fear, 'I embrace change'. Learning new things as we get older is important in order to keep that grey

matter going and stave off degeneration. Try something new – learn the piano or Zumba or Chinese. I'm going to learn how to kitesurf next.

Nicholas Parsons, actor and entertainer

I have to [exercise] or I'd fall over. Every morning I go through a sequence of stretching exercises. I force myself before breakfast.

Helen Mirren, actress

It's hard to let go of our business, of the creativity involved. It's also hard to let go of the attention. You don't think that you're addicted or in love with that attention, you think it doesn't mean anything to you, until suddenly you don't get it.

Mary Berry, chef and TV presenter

This is one of the most exciting times of my life – and how many other people at the age of 678 are able to say that!

Julia Crosthwait, model

I think [ageing] is fabulous! I don't have men hitting on me. I can say outrageous things and people just laugh. I've got lots of life's big events out of the way so now I feel a real sense of freedom. ... As long as my health is good and I can play tennis and move around, I really don't have a problem getting older. And if I suddenly couldn't move well any more, I have lots of books I've waited 61 years to read.

Marilyn Monroe, movie star

We should all start to live before we get too old. Fear is stupid. So are regrets.

Ingrid Tarrant, broadcaster

People ask me how I'll be in 20 years. The answer is that I'll be just like I am now. I expect my children will have finally moved out but that a gang of my friends will have moved in. We'll pool our resources and employ a driver and a cook and a housekeeper and then have a completely fabulous time.

June Whitfield, actress

> So long as people are good enough to ask and so long as I am capable of doing it, I'll be there. I love working. It gives you a reason to get up in the morning.

Piers Morgan, celebrity interviewer

> What do I plan to do it in my retirement? Same as I do now – drink, moan and eat a lot of cheese.

Norman Wisdom, comic actor

> You know you're getting old when a four-letter word for something pleasurable two people can do in bed together is R-E-A-D.

Will Rogers, American comedian and actor

> Eventually you will reach a point when you stop lying about your age and start bragging about it.

Pablo Picasso, artist

> We don't grow older, we grow riper.

Bertrand Russell, philosopher

> The whiter my hair becomes, the more ready people are to believe what I say.

Benjamin Franklin, US statesman

> Life's tragedy is that we get old too soon and wise too late.

Oscar Wilde, dramatist

> When I was young, I thought that money was the most important thing in life; now that I am old, I know it is.

Charles M Schulz, US cartoonist

> Just remember, once you're over the hill, you begin to pick up speed.

Muhammad Ali, boxer

> The man who views the world at 50 the same as he did at 20 has wasted 30 years of his life.

The Queen Mother

> Don't retouch my wrinkles in the photograph. I would not want it to be thought that I had lived for all these years without having anything to show for it.

Clement Freud, broadcaster

> There is no law that decrees when not to whinge, but you reach a certain age – 80 seems about right – when you're expected to manifest querulousness – the coffee's too hot, the boiled egg's too soft ...

Sir Edward Grey, politician

> I am getting to an age when I can enjoy the last sport left. It is called hunting for your spectacles.

Peter Cook, comedian

> I keep fit. Every morning, I do 100 laps of an Olympic-sized swimming pool – in a small motor launch.

Helen Hayes, American actress

> If you rest, you rust.

Norman Wisdom, comic actor

> As you get older three things happen. The first is your memory goes, and I can't remember the other two...

Chapter 11

Bringing it all together
The blueprint for a psychologically sound retirement

Retirement can be seen as a crisis; if seen instead as a challenge there is more likely to be a positive outcome. Throughout this book we have guided you towards a new form of retirement. We have looked at the challenges of retirement, given you a number of strategies and made a lot of suggestions.

In summary, here's our handy blueprint for you to follow.

Planning ahead

If you fail to plan ahead, retirement will come as quite a shock! Shock can trigger adverse health events/problems, so to best avoid this you need to plan ahead.

- Acquire and develop interests and skills over time. Think about these before you retire so you can start those now.
- Develop social networks around your interests – this may take time.
- Get others around you used to your new activities. Do this by drawing up a list; speak to others; consider what you can continue with.
- Talk to others about your plans and goals and work within their needs/expectations.

Start saving

Financial planning for retirement should begin the moment you start work. How many of us actually plan our career development, let along our lifetime financial development?

The sooner you start to save the better! It might be too late for you, but you can now start a pension for your child or grandchild from birth. The government contributes 25 per cent up to a certain point, and it can't be withdrawn before age 55.

Prepare for old age

Things to think about:

- dependency;
- financial stress;
- degeneration of body and mind;
- the potential strain on your relationship(s); and
- loss.

Your 20-point retirement blueprint

1. Communicate openly with loved ones, friends, ex-colleagues.
2. Contribute – play an active role in your community.
3. Belong – foster affiliation wherever possible; socialise.
4. Give – involvement in other people's lives will reciprocated.
5. Learn – don't stop – acquire new skills or ideas, even for fun.
6. Eat well and healthily; watch your weight and alcohol intake.
7. Have regular medical check-ups; be proactive about your health.
8. Exercise regularly (relaxing; good for physical and mental health, social).
9. Don't put up with mental health problems (low mood, depression, anxiety, addictions, phobias or fears).
10. Get support in the face of overwhelming grief or loss.
11. Accept retirement brings change and, with age, limitations.
12. Have a philosophy or set of beliefs that will guide and sustain you.
13. Have goals and plan, but adapt these if required.
14. Identify hobbies and interests and get them under way sooner rather than later.
15. Realise your dreams (keep fantasies as fantasies).
16. Avoid gambling and other addictive behaviours.
17. Avoid hazardous situations.
18. Challenge negative thoughts; have a positive mindset.
19. Maintain a strong focus on socialising, seeking out fun and happy people.
20. Take advice on financial and legal issues.

We wish you a very happy and healthy life after work.

Resources

Further reading

Lara Aknin et al. From Wealth to Well-Being? Money Matters but Less than People Think, *The Journal of Positive Psychology* 4(6) (2009), 523–527.

Richard Benson, *Old Git Wit, Quips and Quotes for the Young at Heart* (Summersdale, 2013).

Barbara Bloomfield, *Couples Therapy: Dramas of Love and Sex* (McGraw Hill, 2013).

David D. Burns, *Feeling Good: The New Mood Therapy* (Morrow & Co., 1980).

David D. Burns, *The Feeling Good Handbook*, 2nd edition (Plume, 2000).

David D. Burns, *Feeling Good Together: The Secret to Making Troubled Relationships Work* (Harmony, 2010).

Gene Cohen, *The Mature Mind: The Positive Power of the Ageing Brain* (Basic Books, 2005).

Colin Espie, *Overcoming Sleep Difficulties and Insomnia: A Self-help Guide Using Cognitive Behavioural Techniques*, 2nd edition (Robinson, 2019).

Friends of the Elderly, *The Future of Loneliness* (Friends of the Elderly, 2015), available at www.fote.org.uk/publications/2015/06/16/future-loneliness-report

International Longevity Centre–UK, *Europe's Ageing Demography: An ILC-UK 2014 EU Factpack* (ILC, 2014), available at www.ilcuk.org.uk/index.php/publications/publication_details/europes_ageing_demography

International Longevity Centre–UK, *A Better Offer: The future of volunteering in an ageing society* (ILC, 2014), available at www.ilcuk.org.uk/index.php/publications/publication_details/a_better_offer_the_future_of_volunteering_in_an_ageing_society

Kevin Meares and Mark Freeston, *Overcoming Worry and Generalised Anxiety Disorder: A Self-help Guide Using Cognitive Behavioural Techniques*, 2nd edition (Robinson, 2015).

Michael J. Poulin, Stephanie L. Brown, Amanda J. Dillard and Dylan M. Smith, Giving to Others and the Association Between Stress and Mortality, *American Journal of Public Health* 103(9) (2013), 1649–1655.

Constance Reid and Oliver Mellors, *A Sex God's/Goddess's Guide to People with Back Pain* (Backcare, 2011), available at www.backcare.org.uk

Fran Smith, Carina Eriksen and Robert Bor, *Coping with the Psychological Effects of Illness: Strategies to Manage Anxiety and Depression* (Sheldon Press, 2015).

Stuart Turner, *Haynes Retirement Manual: A No-Nonsense Guide to a Happy and Healthy Retirement* (Haynes, 2015).

Organisations and links

Age UK (0800 055 6112, www.ageuk.org.uk) – information and advice, and support for independence and against loneliness

Alzheimer's Research UK (www.alzheimersresearchuk.org/about-dementia) – information about dementia

Anchor (0808 102 4070, www.anchor.org.uk) – care and housing for people who are aged 55+

Blue Cross (www.bluecross.org.uk) – offers opportunities for volunteering

Carers Trust (info@carers.org, www.carers.org)

Coffee Companions (0845 003 0630, www.coffeecompanions.co.uk) – chat mats make it easier to start conversations in public places

Contact the Elderly (www.contact-the-elderly.org.uk) – tea parties to combat loneliness

Dementia UK: www.dementiauk.org

First Stop (info@firststopcareadvice.org, www.firststopcareadvice.org.uk) – the first point of contact for any issues relating to care of the elderly

Friends of the Elderly (020 7730 8263, enquiries@fote.org.uk, www.fote.org.uk) – supporting older people

Home Improvement Agencies (www.findmyhia.org.uk/) – list of Home improvement and handyperson service providers

Housing Care (0800 377 7070, www.housingcare.org) – free advice on care for older people, including residential homes, and homesharing schemes listed by county (www.housingcare.org/service/type-30-homesharing.aspx). See their new Housing Options for Older People information service

Independent Age (0800 319 6789, www.independentage.org) – support and advice helpline, including a befriending service

Marriage Care (0800 389 3801, https://www.marriagecare.org.uk/) help couples build and sustain strong, fulfilling and healthy relationships, and provide support for relationship difficulties.

National Benevolent Institution (01666 505 500, office@natben.org.uk https://natben.org.uk/) – provides financial assistance to help people live with dignity and in comfort

National Trust (www.nationaltrust.org.uk).

NBFA Assisting the Elderly (www.nbfa.org.uk) – for help with independent living and support for carers

NHS Choices guide to dementia (www.nhs.uk/Conditions/dementia-guide/Pages/causes-of-dementia.aspx)

Relate (enquiries@relate.org.uk, https://www.relate.org.uk/) gives relationship support to everyone

Pension Credits (0800 99 1234, www.gov.uk/pension-credit/how-to-claim)
Retired and Senior Volunteering Programme (RSVP) (csv-rsvp.org.uk)
Revitalise (0303 303 0145, www.revitalise.org.uk) – respite holidays for people with disabilities and carers
Royal Voluntary Service (0845 608 0122, www.royalvoluntaryservice.org.uk) – enriches the lives of older people
Saga (www.saga.co.uk) – holidays, insurance, investment services
Samaritans (08457 909090 www.samaritans.org.uk) run a 24-hour helpline
The Silver Line (0800 470 8090, www.thesilverline.org.uk) – a free confidential helpline providing information, advice and friendship, including letters
Silver Sunday (020 7641 3609, info@silversunday.org.uk, www.silversunday.org.uk) – an annual event to celebrate older people and combat loneliness
Solicitors for the Elderly (0844 567 6173, admin@sfe.legal, www.sfe.legal) – solicitors, barristers, and chartered legal executives who provide specialist legal advice for older and vulnerable people, their families and carers
Tax Help for Older People (0845 601 3321, www.taxvol.org.uk) – from the charity Tax Volunteers, a free, independent and expert help service for older people on lower incomes
Turn2us (0808 802 2000, www.turn2us.org.uk) – access to benefits and grants, including a helpline
University of the Third Age (U3A) (020 8466 6139, www.u3a.org.uk) – for learning together in local groups
Which? Elderly Care (www.which.co.uk/elderly-care) – practical advice about elderly care choices

Index

addictions 57–62
adjustment 22
Age UK 11, 56
ageing 5, 8, 27–39, 84–95
alcohol 5, 57–62, 74, 83
altruism 33–6, 35; see also mentoring
American Association for the Advancement of Science 54
anger 50
annuity 99
anxiety 20, 21, 41, 42, 47, 64
assumptions 13–14
attention 22

behaviour 19, 41
blame 45, 50
blood sugar 92–3
blueprint 108
bereavement 49–50
boredom 48
brain 27–39, 90–1; training 31

caring 32; trap 82–3
catastrophising 49
change: fear of 18–19; management 12, 19
cognitive behavioural therapy 42, 45
coping strategies 39, 48, 51, 53, 54, 60
cost of living 10
creativity 31, 95; see also hobbies

dementia 29–30
denial 50
Department of Work and Pensions 9

depression 50
divorce 75
dog owners 95

emotional reasoning 45
emotions 23–6, 62–5
equities 100
exercise 22, 23, 37, 47–8, 85–90; and low mood 64
expectations 9, 14–15, 26

fatigue 50
fear 20–2, 42–8
Filkin report 7–8
finances 7, 49, 96–102
fitness 31–2
food 91–4
Friends of the Elderly 53, 56

gambling 5
gender 73
grief 49–50; see also loss

Harvard School of Public Health 88
headaches 51
health 6, 7, 84–95
hobbies 21, 31, 36–7, 49, 63, 72
Huffington Post 81

identity 11
insomnia see sleep
International Longevity Centre 8, 9

labelling 44–5
learning 28–9, 31, 32

Index

legacy 13
loneliness 53–7
longevity 4, 5–8, 33, 95
loss 49–50, 62, 63, 77
low mood 48, 64

maturation 20–9
Mediterranean diet 92
mental health 1, 5; tips 38–9
metabolism 29
mentoring 34
mindfulness 22, 48; eating 93
mobility 85–90
Money Advice Service 83
mood 43, 48–9

National Insurance 97
negative thoughts 14–15
neighbours 55
nutrition 91–4

Office of National Statistics 83

pension 79, 97
physical symptoms 50–1
play 36–7
positive thoughts 14–15
Prince's Initiative for Mature Enterprise 81
psychological problems 2
psychological therapy 40–62, 63–5
psychology 12–26

Relate 76
relationships 66–76; tips 72

relaxation 22, 47
Royal Voluntary Service 56
running 89

saving 9, 22, 96–102, 107
self-employment 78
separateness 72
sex 73
sleep 19, 27, 39; insomnia, 51–3; apnoea 52
smiling 64
social media 55
sport 36–7, 38, 88
stamina 88–9
status 77
strength 86–8
stress, 40–62, 63–5, 66–72

tax 101
thinking errors 17–18
tracking 94
trustee 34

uncertainty 64
unemployment 80
unhappiness 64–5
University of the Third Age 56

vitamins 93; see also nutrition
volunteering 32–4, 82

wellbeing 4–5, 49, 67, 84–5, 95
work 6, 77–83
worry 13–14, 15, 17, 22, 41–2, 45; and sleep 52–3

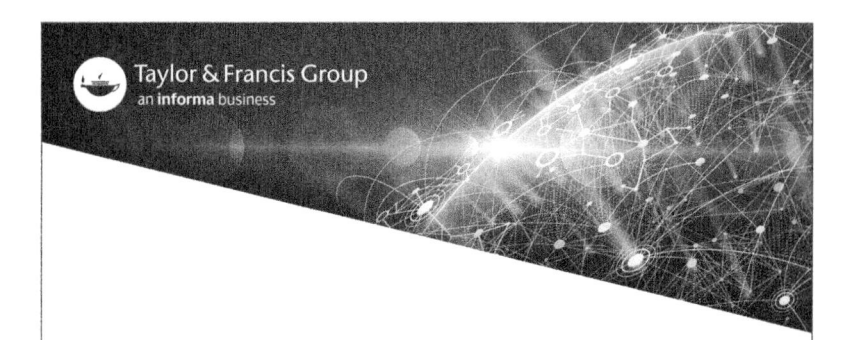